# 1,000,000 Books

are available to read at

# Forgotten Books

www.ForgottenBooks.com

Read online
Download PDF
Purchase in print

ISBN 978-1-331-66255-6
PIBN 10219531

This book is a reproduction of an important historical work. Forgotten Books uses state-of-the-art technology to digitally reconstruct the work, preserving the original format whilst repairing imperfections present in the aged copy. In rare cases, an imperfection in the original, such as a blemish or missing page, may be replicated in our edition. We do, however, repair the vast majority of imperfections successfully; any imperfections that remain are intentionally left to preserve the state of such historical works.

Forgotten Books is a registered trademark of FB &c Ltd.
Copyright © 2018 FB &c Ltd.
FB &c Ltd, Dalton House, 60 Windsor Avenue, London, SW19 2RR.
Company number 08720141. Registered in England and Wales.

For support please visit www.forgottenbooks.com

# 1 MONTH OF FREE READING

at

www.ForgottenBooks.com

---

By purchasing this book you are eligible for one month membership to ForgottenBooks.com, giving you unlimited access to our entire collection of over 1,000,000 titles via our web site and mobile apps.

To claim your free month visit:
www.forgottenbooks.com/free219531

\* Offer is valid for 45 days from date of purchase. Terms and conditions apply.

English
Français
Deutsche
Italiano
Español
Português

# www.forgottenbooks.com

**Mythology** Photography **Fiction**
Fishing Christianity **Art** Cooking
Essays Buddhism Freemasonry
Medicine **Biology** Music **Ancient Egypt** Evolution Carpentry Physics
Dance Geology **Mathematics** Fitness
Shakespeare **Folklore** Yoga Marketing
**Confidence** Immortality Biographies
Poetry **Psychology** Witchcraft
Electronics Chemistry History **Law**
Accounting **Philosophy** Anthropology
Alchemy Drama Quantum Mechanics
Atheism Sexual Health **Ancient History**
**Entrepreneurship** Languages Sport
Paleontology Needlework Islam
**Metaphysics** Investment Archaeology
Parenting Statistics Criminology
**Motivational**

ANTIQUITIES
OF THE
PRIORY
OF
GREAT MALVERN

PORCH OF MALVERN PRIORY.

LONDON.

THE LIBRARY
OF
THE UNIVERSITY
OF CALIFORNIA
LOS ANGELES

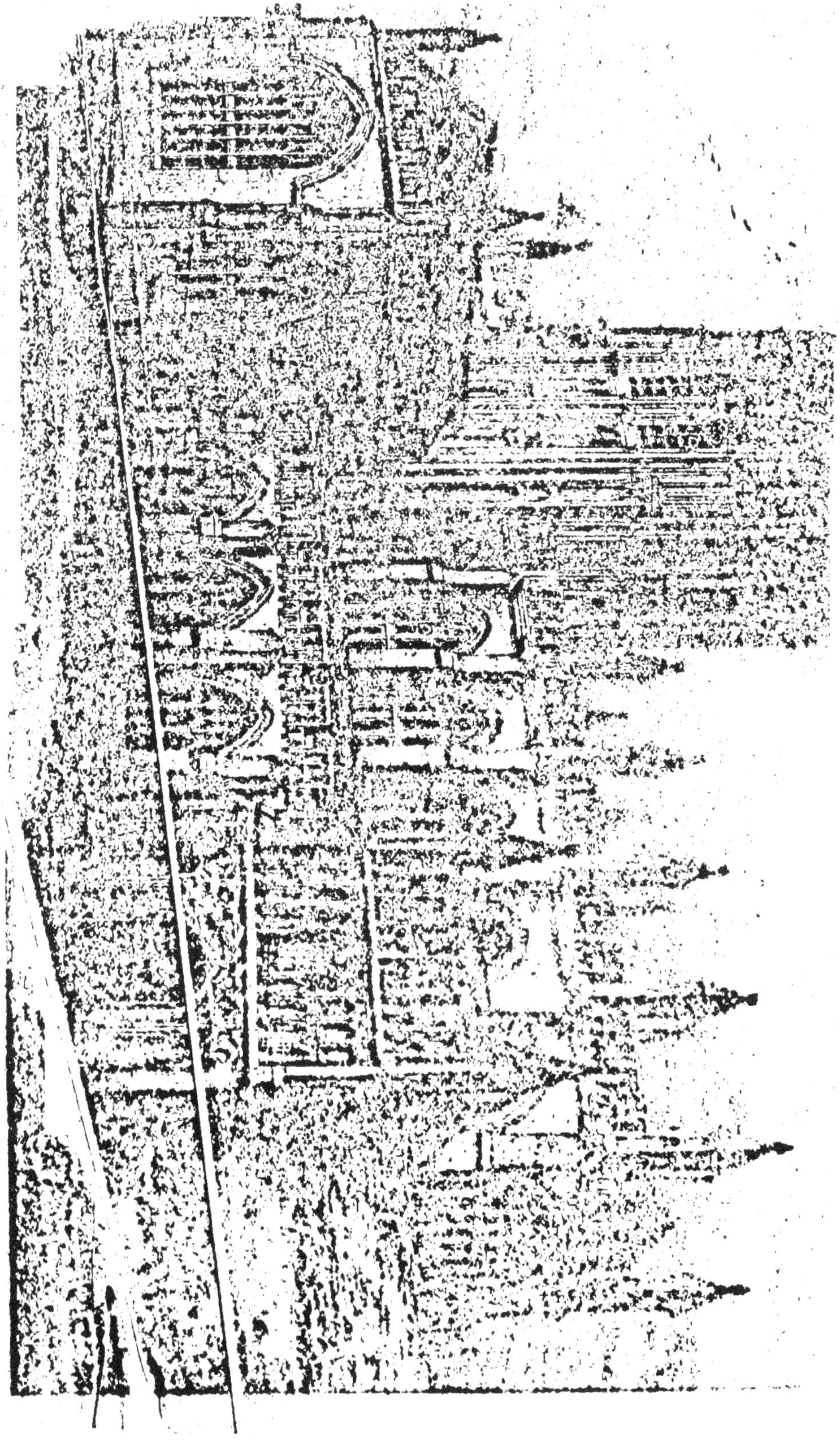

To the exemplary and venerable

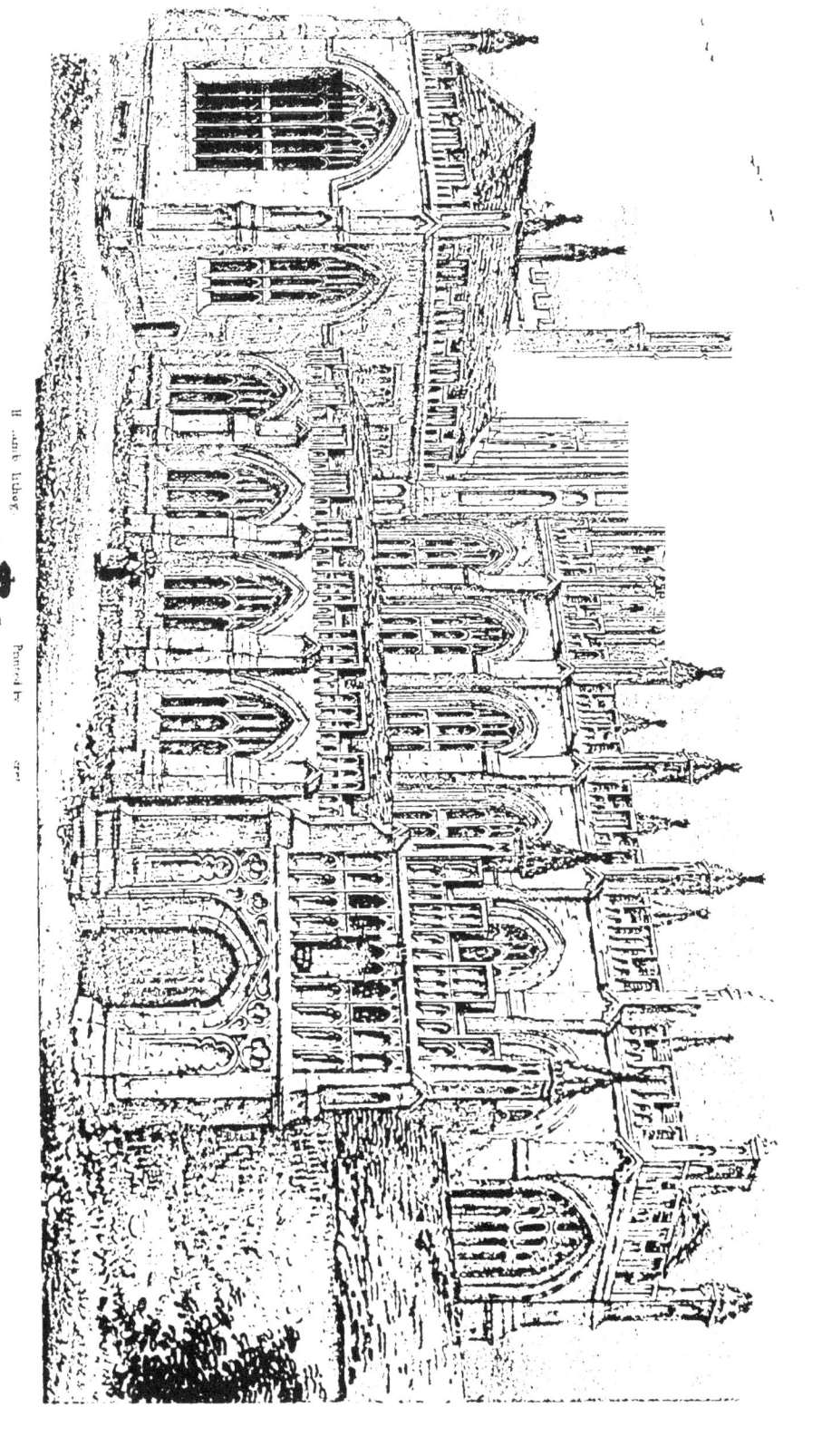

# DISSERTATION

ON THE

## ANTIQUITIES

OF THE

# PRIORY OF GREAT MALVERN,

IN

## WORCESTERSHIRE.

BY THE

REV. H. CARD, D.D. F.A.S. &c. &c. &c.

VICAR OF GREAT MALVERN.

―――― And O, ye swelling hills, and spacious plains!
Besprent from shore to shore with steeple towers,
And spires whose " silent finger points to heaven ;"
Nor wanting at wide intervals the bulk
Of ancient Minster, lifted above the cloud
Of the dense air which town or city breeds
To intercept the sun's glad beams,—may ne'er
That true succession fail of English hearts,
Who with ancestral feeling, can perceive
What in those holy structures ye possess
Of ornamental interest, and the charm
Of pious sentiment diffused afar,
And human charity, and social love.—WORDSWORTH.

Nor rough, nor barren, are the winding ways
Of hoar antiquity, but strewn with flowers.—WARTON.

## LONDON:

PRINTED FOR J. G. & F. RIVINGTON,

ST. PAUL'S CHURCH YARD, AND WATERLOO PLACE, PALL MALL;

& SOLD BY RIDGE, WORCESTER.

1834.

LONDON:
GILBERT AND RIVINGTON, PRINTERS,
ST. JOHN'S-SQUARE.

# DEDICATION.

TO HER ROYAL HIGHNESS

## THE DUCHESS OF KENT.

MADAM,

My pleasing labour is now finished; for pleasing I can truly call it, since it was undertaken at the desire of your Royal Highness, graciously communicated to me on a recent occasion. I am far from thinking my performance perfect, but do not imagine any thing I can add of sufficient value to require longer delay in placing it before your Royal Highness, with every sentiment of profound respect.

I have the honor to remain,

MADAM,

Your Royal Highness' most obliged,

and most dutiful Servant,

HENRY CARD.

THE VICARAGE,
*September* 8, 1834.

# PRIORY OF GREAT MALVERN,

IN

## WORCESTERSHIRE.

---

IF antiquity impart additional dignity to the temple as well as to the palace—and what acute observer of the human mind will dispute this fact?—then must those Christian edifices reared by the pious munificence of our forefathers excite our deepest reverence, and call forth our most fervent aspirations for their preservation. Unquestionably he who has perused the frightful accounts unfolded at the Visitations of the Abbeys—the detestable crimes practised in those cloisters of iniquity and impurity[1],—cannot but acknowledge that Henry VIII.,

[1] " I know not by what right," observes Mr. Hallam, " we should disbelieve the reports of the visitation under Henry VIII. entering, as they do, into a multitude of specific charges, both probable in their nature, and consonant to the unanimous opinion of the world." Middle Ages, vol. iii. p. 352, 353. For additional confirmation of these assertions, see Fosbrooke's British Monachism, vol. i. p. 127, where that writer has thoroughly exposed the delinquencies of the Monks. But nothing can be more indisputable than the fact, that the monasteries were the chief or sole preservers of the historical Memorials of their times, however just may be the remark of Gibbon, " that of such manuscripts, the casualty of fire, or the slow progress of damp and worms, would often endanger their limited and precarious existence." See his Miscellaneous Works, vol. ii. p. 709. We learn from Spelman, that some sympathy for the fate of the

in their suppression, rendered an essential service to the cause of true religion. Glorious as the era of the Reformation was, still it will be ever matter of regret to the real lovers of the fine arts, whether Roman Catholic or Protestant, that so many stately Abbeys, monuments of the skill as well as the piety of our ancestors, should have been demolished or dilapidated. Among, however, those national ornaments which escaped the hand of destruction, the conventual church of Great Malvern still retains most of its original perfection. Occupying a spot as lovely as the eye ever rested upon, and built after the customary form of a cross, this venerable structure, in its magnitude, proportions, and decorations, with its dark grey tower so full of impression and effect,—with its pierced battlements and graceful pinnacles,— presents a most beautiful specimen of that florid style of English architecture which prevailed in the reign of Henry VII. The whole length of this majestic and picturesque fabric, as given by Mr. Chambers in his History of Great Malvern[1], is an hundred and seventy-one feet, its breadth sixty-three feet. The height of the nave is sixty-three feet; and that of the tower a hundred and twenty-four feet. Congreve must have had a building

---

Monks and Nuns was felt on the part of the Commons, as Henry was obliged to send for them, and to declare, in his usual bluff manner, that if the Bill were not passed, which put him and his heirs in possession of all monastic establishments, with the property belonging to them, both real and personal, he would cause some of their heads to be struck off. History of Sacrilege, p. 183.

[1] P. 53. Before the demolition of the South Transept Aisle, and of the Lady Chapel, at the east end of the church, which Cole the antiquary states to have been about fifty feet in length, (see MSS. Brit. Mus. vol. x. folio 119), the building must have been quite cathedral-like in appearance. Well, indeed, may Cole style it, "a most noble structure." The old parish church was dedicated to St. Thomas the Apostle, and stood near the present church, at the north-west corner of the church-yard. Its length was ninety feet, its breadth thirty-six, and it had one small chapel to the south. See Thomas. Antiq. Priorat. Majoris Malverne, p. xci.

of this sort in his mind, when, in that noble passage of his Tragedy, he exclaims,—

> " How reverend is the face of this tall pile,
> Whose ancient pillars rear their marble heads
> To bear aloft its arched and ponderous roof,
> By its own weight made stedfast and immoveable,
> Looking tranquillity [1]."

In the middle ages [2] art commenced with sacred subjects. Indeed, ecclesiastical architecture was the chief boast of those dark times. Churches, therefore, independently of early religious associations, must always be objects of great interest, as they illustrate our history, and the state of the arts at the time in which they were erected. It is painful then to remark, that, after such a lavish prodigality of expenditure, we have so few beautiful new Churches to compensate for the loss and decay of the proud fanes of olden times. While these fill the beholder with awe, admiration, and delight, there is nothing in those to raise the mind to a loftier state of thought and feeling; the latter—sublime structures, and therefore awakening sublime emotions,—are as distinguished for their vastness, grandeur and science, as the former are devoid of such qualities or attributes.

Unfortunately, our present system of education pays little or no attention to art; or that great desideratum in our Universities, a Professorship of Ecclesiastical Architecture from the era of the Norman Conquest to that of the Reformation,—a period in which is exhibited such boundless variety in all the different gradations of style,—would long ago have contributed not only to form the national taste upon

[1] Mourning Bride, Act ii. Scene 1.
[2] According to the authority of Mr. Hallam, and no higher can be produced on the subject, the Middle Ages comprise about one thousand years, from the invasion of France by Clovis, to that of Naples by Charles VIII. Vol. iii. p. 308.

purer principles, but might have drawn the notice of the Government to the better preservation of those highly interesting edifices which have not sunk under the ruthless fury of the fanatic, or the more silent operations of Time.

Formerly, upon this subject, there was an intensity of religious feeling, instead of that obtusity which has been for so many years past but too apparent on the part of those who have directed the movements of the State. No stronger proof of this assertion can be afforded, than that Sir Reginald Bray, the restorer of the Priory, a brief history of which we are about to give, was, to use the parliamentary phrase of this day, the *Premier* of Henry VII. His memory is immortalized by the unrivalled skill and taste displayed by him in the construction of Henry's Chapel at Westminster, "that glorious work of fine intelligence [1]," and in the completion of that of St. George's in Windsor Castle. The other points in his character entitle him to an honourable renown. It was the complaint of a great statesman and historian[2], "that we are often declaiming about the wisdom of our ancestors, without knowing what they mean, or hardly ever citing any particulars of their conduct or of their dicta." That we may not commit the error here censured, we will show in what a brilliant light Sir Reginald's character is set by an ancient writer.

[1] The pretensions of Alcock, Bishop of Ely, have been advanced as a participator with Sir Reginald, on this memorable occasion. But this is pure assumption with many. We believe, that the evidence of Sir Reginald being the architect of this *wonder of the world*, as it has been styled, will stand the strictest examination. There is just cause for regret, that we are still without any certain or accurate knowledge upon the subject of the other edifices constructed by him. "It is surprising," observes Mr. Britton, "that more particulars of this truly eminent man, and of the public buildings he is said to have designed, have not been satisfactorily developed." Architectural Antiquities, vol. iii. p. 34, 35.

[2] See Correspondence of the late Gilbert Wakefield, B.A. with the late Right Honourable Charles Fox, p. 86.

"After the death of this noble Princess Elizabeth, departed Sir Reginalde Braye, Knight of the Garter, a very ffather of his country, a sage and grave person, and a fervent lover of justice. Insomuch that if any things had been done against good law or equitie, he would, after an humble fashyon, reprehende the Kinge, and gyve him good advertysement how to reform that offence, and to be more circumspect in another like case. Of the same vertue and honest plainness was John Moreton, Archbyshop of Canterbury, which died two years before. So these two persons were over restrayned of the Kinge's wilful scope and unbridled liberties: whereas the rude and ignoraunt people say and affirm that theyr counsaile infected and corrupted the Kinges clean and immaculate conscience contrary to his princely disposition and naturall inclination. Such is ever the errour of the common people: but surely as longe as the Kinge would heare and obeye such as warned him of his office royall and kingly duetie, he could in no wise erre or swarve aside [1]."

In thus recording the courageous wisdom and public virtue of this pillar of the state—for Sir Reginald shone as a soldier as well as a counsellor—we shall so far testify our respect for the observation just quoted, as to give a few more particulars respecting this most liberal benefactor, or to speak more correctly, second founder of the Priory. The place of his nativity was St. John's Bedwardine[2], in Worcestershire, and he entered into public life with many of the external advantages of birth and fortune. His ancestors came to England with William the Conqueror. Sir Richard, the father of Sir Reginald,

---

[1] See MS. Lansdowne, Mus. Brit. No. 978; Bishop Kennet's Collections, fol. 262. 1503.

[2] Some writers represent him to have been a native of Great Malvern; but others, who are better informed on the subject, agree with Nash, that he was born in the parish above mentioned, in 1st Richard III. 1483.

and, according to some, physician to Henry VI. was of Eaton Bray, in the county of Bedford, and endeared himself so much to the King, as to be sworn of the Privy Council. Sir Reginald early gained the good opinion of Margaret, Countess of Richmond and Derby, and ultimately became a chief instrument in assisting her son, Henry, to mount the English throne. Great undertakings require great qualifications and abilities. And when that master-stroke of policy—the union of the two Houses of York and Lancaster, by the marriage of Henry with Elizabeth, daughter of Edward IV. was projected by the Duke of Buckingham, and Moreton, Bishop of Ely, they fixed on Sir Reginald as the person to carry it into execution. In these words did Moreton specify his merits to the Duke. " He is sober, secret, and well-witted, and his prudent policy is known to encompass things of great importance." The firmness, temper, and address of Sir Reginald, in an enterprise where so many discordant feelings and embroiled interests were concerned, led finally to complete success: for he drew over to the cause of his mistress, Sir Giles D'Aubeny, Sir John Cheyney, and other persons of great weight in the kingdom. As a reward for having acted so prominent a part in this transaction, Henry, at his accession, loaded him with estates and offices of large profit. In 1494, he was elected High Steward of Oxford ; and he did not disappoint the hopes of that learned body in maintaining their rights and privileges. Henry, in his letters-patent to his said Steward, knight of his body, recognising, no doubt at Sir Reginald's urgent solicitation, the franchises of the University, as including, besides other matters, the right of hearing the criminal causes of scholars and other privileged persons, accepted the nomination, and allowed him and his other assessors (named in the patent) or any two of them, to proceed in the common form against offenders. On the marriage of Prince Arthur, the dowry of the Princess was guaranteed to her by the Duke of York, the two Archbishops, the Bishops of Winchester and Lincoln, and Sir Reginald Bray. The eminent services which he had rendered to Henry procured him also the dignities of Knight of the Garter, and Chancellor of the Duchy of Lancaster. Bred a soldier as well as a politician, his skill and gallantry were conspicuously displayed in the decisive battle of Bosworth Field, and in that of Blackheath, where the Cornish insurgents were completely routed. In short, placed in employments which he executed with equal ability and integrity, it was his rare good fortune to enjoy uninterruptedly the favour of one of the most sagacious and sternest Monarchs that ever held the British sceptre. Sir Reginald died on the 5th of August, 1502-3, and was buried in the middle of a Chapel at Windsor, which was founded by him, and still bears his name: and Churton, summing up his character, says, " that he received from the Crown innumerable patents, marks of favour, grants of emolument, which, as they did not corrupt, served only to display the integrity of the senator and the statesman: while his counsel carried so great a sway with the court, that, had he not died before Henry, the acts of rapacity and oppression with which that Monarch's later annals are disgraced, would no doubt have been less numerous and less flagrant, if not entirely prevented[1]."

According to Bishop Tanner and Dr. Nash, the Priory of Great Malvern first rises into notice from a very remote period. The former says, " here in the great wild forest was an hermitage, or some kind of religious house for seculars, before the Conquest, with some en-

---

[1] The most authentic information of Sir Reginald Bray will be found in Dugdale's Baronage; Kippis's Edit. of the Biog. Brit. art. Bray; Churton's Lives of the Founders of Brazen-nose College; and Manning's Surrey.

dowment by the gift of King Edward the Confessor;" and the latter, speaking of Malvern in his Collections for the History of Worcestershire, observes, " Before the Conquest it was a wilderness thick set with trees, in the midst of which some monks, who aspired to greater perfection, retired from the Priory of Worcester, and became hermits. The enthusiasm spread so fast that the number soon increased to three hundred, when, forming themselves into a society, they agreed to live according to the order of St. Benedict, and elected Aldwin, one of their number, to be superior. Thus was the monastery founded about the year 1083, with the consent and approbation of St. Wolstan, Bishop of Worcester." It was dedicated to the Virgin Mary and also to St. Michael, as we learn from an original charter preserved in the British Museum [1].

In the Annales Wigornienses, we are expressly told that Aldwin was the founder of the Malvern Monastery, A.D. 1085. William of Malmesbury has furnished us with a somewhat detailed account of the circumstances which induced him to commence the undertaking. What person at the present day does not feel a peculiar pleasure, especially if he have an archaic [2] tone of mind, when satiated with our profitless philosophizing, he turns to the simple but graphic tales

---

[1] See Dugdale's Monast. Angl. N.E. Part xxii. p. 440.

[2] Whether any of our readers be possessed with the feelings and sentiments we are now about to speak of, would puzzle us as much to determine as a dubious case of law: but we have known those who entirely participate in them; to whom the study of the dusty record and the mildewed charter has the same inexpressible charms as the sweet chirpings of birds in woods and fields, the soft rippling of streams, and the rude whistling of the winds, have for others. " I have heard one of the greatest geniuses this age has produced, who had been trained up in all the polite studies of antiquity, assure me, upon his being obliged to search into several rolls and records, that, notwithstanding such an employment was at first very dry and irksome to him, he at last took an incredible pleasure in it, and preferred it even to the reading of Virgil or Cicero." Spectator, No. 447.

of the good old gossiping chroniclers. For, in that pictorial age, of which we are discoursing, when the manners and opinions of contemporaries were so naturally represented, there was no wide gulf fixed between fancy's regions and those of sober reality; between the dim and tremulous twilight of uncertainty, and the steady effulgence of conviction, but annalists and their readers—rari nantes in gurgite vasto[1],—were alike content to wander on in " the palpable obscure" of the time, yielding unhesitating confidence to its delusions and its dreams. Whenever the writer is firmly assured of what he relates, his narrations generally bear an impress of truth to others. Indeed he demands, and expects their faith in all that he propounds, as if what he had ascertained to his own conviction was equally clear to them. Such a national Chronicler was William, the Monk of Malmesbury; for in his day the literary man was only to be found in the monastery. None then handled the pen to any useful or edifying purpose, but the member of a chapter or of a convent[2]. The following

---

[1] " The gross mass of the laity, from the baron to the mechanic, were then more addicted to the exercises of the body than to those of the mind. Few among them could read, still fewer could write: none were acquainted with the Latin tongue; and if they sometimes listened to a tale of past times, their puerile love of the marvellous would prefer the romance of Sir Launcelot, or Sir Tristram, to the authentic narratives most honourable to their country and their ancestors." See Gibbon's Address upon the Study of the History and Antiquities of Great Britain; Memoirs, vol. ii. p. 709. But even at the end of the sixteenth century, the ignorance and barbarism of the times were such, that Marlow, " he of mighty line," makes one of the clowns, in his tragedy of Faustus, say to another, " Snail, what hast thou got there, *a book?* why thou can'st not tell ne'er a word on't."

[2] And not many there either. Parchment was an article of great expense, from its scarcity, in those days, which was another obstacle to the spread of knowledge, and an excuse to so many of the Monks for being content to sit lazily and proudly in their ignorance. Mr. Hallam quotes Warton for the fact, that no parchment could be procured about 1120, for preparing an illuminated copy of the Bible. Middle Ages, vol. iii. p. 333. We shall offer no apology to the curious reader for presenting to him our researches upon

legend, connected with the history of the Priory, may aptly serve as an illustration of the foregoing remarks. Our translation, it will be seen by the learned reader, is almost a literal one.

There was one Aldwin, a monk, who, with a single companion named Guido, lived as a recluse in that very densely wooded chase, which is called Malvern. After long struggles of conscience, Guido considered it absolutely necessary, as the shortest path to glory, to visit Jerusalem, and see the Lord's sepulchre, or meet a blessed death by the hand of the Saracens. Aldwin was disposed to follow his example, but first consulted his spiritual adviser Wolstan. The prelate dissuaded him, and cooled his ardour by saying, " Do not, I beseech thee, Aldwin, go any where, but remain in your place: believe me, you would wonder if you knew what I know; how much God is about to perform through you in that place." The monk having heard this departed, and now remained firm in purpose, and soothed every sorrow by the hope of the prophecy. Nor was it long after that the prophecy hastened to its fulfilment. One after the other successively came, to the number of thirty. Abundant were the stores of provision which flowed in upon them from the neighbouring inhabitants, who judged themselves happy in being permitted to minister aught to God's ser-

---

this subject. Many entries occur in the Wardrobe Accounts of various kings' reigns, and in the Pipe Rolls, duplicates of which are now in the British Museum, of the sums paid for parchment. One of these entries, in the printed Wardrobe Account of the 28th Edward I. p. 54, is Juliane atte Flode, de Wyntonia, pro pergamens empt' de eadem per Jobēm de Langeford pro expens' garde-robe Regis, videlt pro 40 duodenis pergamen' precio duodene 12$d$.—2$l$. 0$s$. 0$d$.—et pro 15 duodenis precio duodene 18$d$.—1$l$. 2$s$. 6$d$. per manus predicte. I. ibidem 15 die Marcii Summa. 3$l$. 2$s$. 6$d$." From this entry it would appear, that 40 dozen skins, at 12$d$. per dozen, cost 2$l$.; and 15 dozen of, perhaps, a superior quality, or larger size, cost 1$l$. 2$s$. 6$d$.; so that parchment must have been sold, in Edward's reign, after the rate of 1$d$. and 1$\frac{1}{2}d$. per skin. In another part of the same Wardrobe Account, (28 Edward I.) 60 dozen skins of parchment, with carriage of same from Lincoln to Westminster, including cordage for packing them, cost 7$l$. 12$s$.

vants; or if there chanced to be need of any thing, they supplied the want by faith, deeming it a little matter to be without carnal food, seeing that they grew fat upon spiritual joys[1]. It would appear, by the following story, that the same Bishop (Wolstan) did not want just vision to discern that the spirits of men must become pure from their errors and vices by first suffering for them, and that without continual training and tutoring, spiritual growth would not proceed in that way so as to be conducive to any permanently good purpose.

One Swelf, a merchant, had been accustomed to visit him once a year to receive his advice in the healing of his spiritual ailments. Once on a time, after giving the absolution, he observed, "You often repeat the sins which you have confessed; because, as the proverb goes, opportunity makes the thief. Wherefore I advise you to become a monk, which, if you do, you will not long have the opportunity for those sins." Upon this, the other rejoined, that he could not possibly become a monk, because he found it so difficult to bring his mind to it. "Go your ways," said the Bishop, in somewhat of a passion; "a monk you will become, whether you choose it or not, but only when the appliances and means of vice have waxen old in you." Which fact we afterwards witnessed, because, when now broken down by old age, and warned by disease, he betook himself to our monastery: but though he had many times repented, yet, nevertheless, as often as any one reminded him of the Bishop's saying, he still laboured to check his temper, and to soften his disposition[2].

In another respect, also, the prediction of this eminent saint[3] of the

---

[1] See Note A, Appendix.  [2] See Note B, Appendix.
[3] "Wilstanus in sanctitate nostro sæculo nomatissimus." Vide Gul. Malm. De Vitis Pontificum, fol. 159. After this quotation we must suppose the mitred priest's pretensions to canonization indisputable: but popular fame is not always to be taken as the best criterion for the honours of saintship. Had some of those worthies, who have been so

monastic calendar (Wolstan) was verified. After Aldwin had procured letters-patent from Pope Gregory VII. and William the Conqueror, Urso d'Abitot, or D'Abtot, a Norman baron, whose property was considerable in this county, as well as other magnates, became a great benefactor to the Priory. It was honoured also in a particular manner by acts of liberality on the part of Henry I., who, besides confirming all former grants, by his Charter, dated 1271, annexed various lands to it. In No. IX. of the Charters and Instruments, in the new edition of Dugdale's Monasticon Anglicanum, are enumerated the possessions, temporal and spiritual, of the Priory, at the period of its taxation by Pope Nicholas IV. 1291.

It was fortunate for the prosperity of this establishment, that Walkerius, or Walcher, its second prior, trod in the steps of the first, in all benevolence to man, and in all humility to God. The zeal of the faithful may well be supposed to have been eager to heap bounty on him, who was so much an object of reverence, that to disbelieve the words of Walcher, was, according to William of Malmesbury, doing an injury to religion[1]. An epitaph is but an imperfect test of merit, but, as an opinion on the worth of individual character, it

---

dignified, lived in the present day, we should naturally conclude that the police officer, or the *cachipollis*, as he is styled in Wiclif's New Testament, (*Dedis of Apostolis*, c. xvi.) would have failed in his duty, if he had not provided his thief-catching apparatus as a means for preventing them from further tainting the community by the badness of their characters. In exemplification of this remark, take the following story of what occurred to St. Martin, as given on the authority of Bellarmine, by Bishop Philpotts. " He had long entertained some pretty strong doubts of the propriety of the devotions offered by the people in his neighbourhood to a supposed saint; because, in truth, there was nothing very certain or satisfactory in the traditions concerning him. One day, when St. Martin was at his prayers, the ghost of this personage appeared to him, and frankly confessed that he was a damned spirit; that when alive, he had been a robber, and that he suffered death for his crimes by the hand of the public executioner." Letters to Butler, p. 35.

[1] ——" cujus verbis qui non credit injuriam religioni facit." De Regibus, &c. &c.

is at least deserving of equal regard with an eulogy on the living. He then must be an epitaph-hater, who would deny that some grains of truth may not lie within the monkish lines inscribed on a stone of coffin-like form in memory of Prior Walcher, which was dug up in May, 1711, in a garden adjoining the church-wall, on the south side of the nave, on which the Priory cloisters were supposed to have stood; a circumstance, be it observed, which gives a sort of warrant to the conjecture that he was buried in them.

> Philosophvs dignvs bonvs Astrologvs, Lotheringvs,
> Vir pivs ac hvmilis, monachvs, Prior hvivs ovilis,
> Hic jacet in cista, Geometricvs ac Abacista,
> Doctor Walchervs; flet plebs, dolet vndiqve clervs;
> Hvic lvx prima mori dedit Octobris seniori;
> Vivat vt in cœlis exoret qvis qve fidelis.   mcxxxv[1].

---

[1] "Here lies entombed Walcherus of Lorraine, Prior of this Convent, noted for his piety and humility, a distinguished Philosopher, a good Astronomer, Geometrician, and Arithmetician; universally lamented by Laity and Clergy. He died on the first day of October, advanced in years. Let every true Christian fervently pray, that he may live in Heaven."—It is a debateable point among the critics, at what period these Latin rhymes made their appearance in the world: and that verses of this kind should be designated *Leonine*, has puzzled the learned Camden himself. "Riming verses, which are called Versus Leoni, *I know not wherefore* (for a lyons taile doth not answer to the middle parts as these verses do), began in the time of Carolus Magnus, and were only in request then and in many ages following, which delighteth in nothing more than in this minstrelsie of meeters." Remains, 1614, p. 337. Might not this name have been given to them after Leo the Great. The whole ancient Roman Liturgy was generally known by the name of the Leonine Sacramentary, though it is believed to have been equally put together by Gelasius I. and by St. Gregory. The monks, in honour of Leo, may likewise have distinguished these verses by his name. Hoarne, in the Preface to his History of Glastonbury, p. xlvi. asserts, that a brass plate was found on the inscription of Walcher's tomb in Great Malvern Church: but, as the lively Walpole says, in his letter to Cole on this subject, "Tom Hearne must have here mistaken brass for stone." Cole's MSS. vol. xxv. fol. 194. We presume that no objection, which will be deemed valid, can be made to the assertion of Cole, "that the use of brass plates for monumental inscriptions was not introduced so early as the time of Henry I."

"My soul delighteth," exclaims the author of Vathek, "in a legendary tale of the monastic sort;" and old Grose, no inconsiderable name among those who are skilled in legendary lore, was used to say to his boon companions, " that he loved a good ghost story, as much as the clown did wrestling and single-stick." Perhaps some of our readers may have the same bent of mind for the marvellous, " for those bodyless creations that ecstacy is very cunning in," and therefore it would be uncourteous in us not to indulge their taste in this respect; especially, as it is incumbent upon us, in our capacity of historiographer to the Priory, not to abbreviate or slur over any circumstance or event, which may revive the long-forgotten reputation of its Superiors. The following story, related to William of Malmesbury by him whose epitaph we have just transcribed, must show in what high estimation he stood with his contemporaries, when this chronicler can invest fancy's air-drawn pictures with all the characters of a real transaction; can consider them as having sufficient warrant to be entitled to a respectful belief, merely because they emanated from the brain of Prior Walcher. "Read not to believe and take for granted," was a piece of advice from Lord Bacon, that would have been thus answered with contumelious scorn in the words of Spenser, by the lovers of the preternatural and visionary.

> " Why then should witless man so much misween
> That nothing is but that which he hath seen."

" Not more than fifteen years have elapsed," said Walcher, "since a contagious disease attacked the Prior of that place, and afterwards destroyed many of the monks. The survivors at first began each to fear for himself, and to pray and to give alms more abundantly than usual: in process of time, however, for such is the nature of man, their fear gradually subsiding, they began to omit them. The cellarer more especially, who publicly and laughingly exclaimed, that the stock of provisions was not adequate to such a consumption as was going on; that he had lately hoped for some reduction of expense, considering there had been so many funerals, but that his hopes were at an end, if the dead consumed what the living could not. It happened on a certain night, when from some urgent business he had deferred going to rest for a long time, that having at length got rid of the difficulties which delayed him, he went towards his dormitory. Singular is the circumstance now to be related. He saw in the Chapter-house the Prior and all who had died that year sitting in the order they had departed, whereat he was affrighted and endeavoured to escape; but was detained by force. Being reproved and corrected after the monastic manner with the scourge, he heard the Prior speak precisely to the following effect :—That it was foolish to be ravenously seeking profit by another's death, seeing that all men were subject to one common fate. That it was impious for a monk who had passed his whole life in the service of the church to be grudged his pittance of pay for a single year after his death: that he himself should die very shortly; but that whatever others might do for him, should redound only to the advantage of those whom he had defrauded: that he might now go, and endeavour to correct by his example those whom he had corrupted by his language. He departed, and demonstrated that he had seen nothing imaginary, as well by the recent marks of the scourging, as by his death, which shortly followed [1]."

Before parting with Malmesbury, we cannot forbear adverting to his apparently earnest desire to take the monastery of Malvern under his especial protection. He is anxious to hold it up to universal

[1] See Note C, Appendix.

respect; though he shows himself not to be the blind and indiscriminate eulogist of it, when he closes his general remarks by saying, in the way of brotherly counsel, that " he hands down this place to immortal hope, while the penury of mortal things distracts and stimulates the monks[1]."

The mitred Abbots of Westminster, ever since the period when Gislibertus Crispinus, one of their number, bestowed several manors and estates upon the Priory, had claimed pre-eminence of power over it. In the reign of Henry II. a violent dispute arose between Richard Ware, Abbot of Westminster, and Godfrey Giffard, Bishop of Worcester, respecting the subordination of Great Malvern. Being both men of inflexible spirit, and of equal energy, the litigation was long protracted; at last Edward I. in the plenary exercise of his royal authority, brought this great cause of contention to an amicable settlement: the Priory being made a grateful offering to the ambition of the Abbot, and the Manor of Knightwick, in this county, given to the Bishop and his successors[2]. But although placed in this instance under the jurisdiction of Westminster, the Prior and Convent appear to have always acted as an independent corporation[3] with respect to the mass of property they had accumulated in the counties of Worcester, Hereford, Gloucester, and Warwick: for the Priors, like

---

[1] ——" Ad immortalem spem commemoro, dum mortalium rerum penuria monachos trahit et animat." De Monasteriis, fol. 162.

[2] For evidence upon these points, vide Regist. chart. et privileg. Abbatiæ Westmonast. MS. Cotton. Mus. Brit. Faustina. A. 111. Malvern, fol. 276. Carta Godefridi Wygorñ epĩ q̃d in cella maiorĩ Malvernie nullam habeat jurisdictionē. C. lxxxv. fol. 276⁶. Composicō int. Westm. & Malverne capit lxxxvj. fol. 277⁶. Rex Edwardus confirmat formam pacis factam in V. Dñm̃. G. Wygorn. Epm. & Westm. sup. cell. Malverñ, cap̃. lxxxvij. fol. 279. Assensus Prioris & Convent.⁹ Malverñ sup ordinacīōn Dm̃ Edwardi Reḡ. cap. lxxxix.

[3] See Tanner's Notitia Monastica.

many others of their order, were desirous of procuring real property by purchase, as well as by charters of donation, though sometimes they alienated their lands in favor of their relations and friends[1].

In 1151, 5 Henry II. William Burdet assigned to Roger, then Prior of Malvern, Avercote or Aucote Monastery, in Warwickshire, as a cell to that Priory. There was also another cell at Brockbury, in the parish of Colwall, Herefordshire. Yet over these, the Abbots of Westminster exercised no sort of control in the disposal of their revenues or appointments. The occasion which led to the foundation of the little monastery of Avecote is quite dramatic as to incident, but, as an atonement for bloodshed, not uncommon in those ferocious times. We shall give this tale to the reader in the direct and simple narrative of Dugdale.

" William Burdet being both a valiant and devout man, made a journey to the Holy Land for subduing of the infidels in those parts, and his steward, whilst he was thus absent, solicited the chastity of his lady, who resisted those his uncivil attempts with much scorn : whereupon he grew so full of envy towards her, that so soon as he had advertisement of his master's arrival in England, he went to meet him ; and to shadow his own foul crime, complained to him of her looseness with others : which false accusation so enraged her husband, that when he came home, and she approached to receive him with joyful embraces, he forthwith mortally stabbed her; and to expiate the same unhappy act, after he understood the truth, he built this monastery[2]."

---

[1] Hanc terram tenuit *Sirof* de Episcopo, tempore Regis Edwardi, quo mortuo dedit Episcopus filiam ejus cum hac terra, cuidam suo militi, qui et mattem pasceret, et Episcopo inde serviret. See Proofs and Illustrations, Part II. p. ccclxvi. in Sir Francis Palgrave's Rise and Progress of the English Commonwealth.

[2] Monas. Angl. p. 455.

18        PRIORY OF GREAT MALVERN.

At the time of the dissolution of religious houses, the Priory was valued, according to Dugdale, at £308. 1s. 5½d., and according to Speed, at £375. 0s. 6½d., Tanner's M. T. Valor and Stevens's Supplement give £307. 1s. 4¾d. as the summa clara. i. e. the net amount. Among its possessions are the manors of Wortefield, Newland, and Powyke, in the county of Worcester, Northwode, in Shropshire, the town of Hatfield, and lands in Baldenhale Malvern, Brannesford and Lye, tithes at Archesfonte, in the diocese of Salisbury, of the yearly value of 40s. The Priory of Malvern had likewise the appropriate churches of Longeney Powyke and Malvern, the patronage of the churches of Hanleye, in the deanry of Powyke, of Upton Snodbury, in the deanry of Pershore, and of Eastleach, in the deanry of Fayrford, in the county of Gloucester[1].

"From the age of Charles Martel," emphatically asks a writer as eloquent as he is profoundly learned, "down to the reigns of Henry, or Joseph, or Napoleon, when could the Pontiff or the Priest retain any possessions which the King and the soldier were determined to acquire[2]?" We are not, therefore, to be surprised, that the domains of this Priory should have shared the fate which befell ecclesiastical possessions more or less in every country in Europe. The level of the ocean changes. Field after field, as wave follows wave, has the Priory been stripped of, by that great innovator Time, to use the often-quoted words of Lord Bacon; so that if one of its monks, who lived in the twelfth or fourteenth century, could now revisit Malvern, he would find all its fair acres alienated or sold[3]; and if he awoke from his

[1] Nash, vol. ii. p. 122, 123.

[2] See the Rise and Progress of the English Commonwealth, by Sir Francis Palgrave, Part I. p. 169.

[3] We learn, upon distinct authority, that Philip and Mary confirmed a purchase made by Henry Fayrefeld, of the manor of Woodfelde, in the county of Worcester, of part of

long slumber with his recollective faculties strong about him, after gazing intently upon that church and well known cross [1], he would,

the lands of the dissolved monastery of Malvern. See Dugdale, Monast. Angl. N. E. p. 444, but into whose hands the other portions of the domain fell, we cannot discover with any certainty.

[1] Crosses, we are told by a writer to whom every student of ecclesiastical architecture is highly indebted, were erected at the entrance of churches, to throw the mind into an attitude of solemn thought and reverence. See Britton on Stone Crosses. May I avail myself of this opportunity (for want of a better) of saying a few words upon some animadversions which have been passed upon me for not removing a cross in the interior of this church. To the prattle of the ignorant, and the sneers of the superficial, I will not throw out a sentence in my defence: but I would endeavour to propitiate those of sounder and more impartial understandings, by addressing them in these lines and note of our great philosophic Poet:

" Yet will we not conceal *the precious cross*,
Like men ashamed.

" The Lutherans have retained the cross within their churches: it is to be regretted that we have not done the same." Wordsworth's Ecclesiastical Sketches, p. 123. Similar sentiments were once expressed to me by the late Mr. Davison—*nomen memorabile*—a name never to be pronounced by low as well as high Churchmen, without a pause of admiration. If moral and intellectual excellences—if orthodoxy without any species of bigotry—if an ardent desire to advance the great cause of Christianity in every quarter of the globe—if a firm attachment to our ecclesiastical establishments, without any hunting after professional honours—if singleness of purpose—if inflexible integrity and extensive charity, without ostentation—be among the best recommendations for a bishopric—as sure they are, or ought to be—then should not this man have died without a mitre on his head. Alas! how many eminent pastors, patterns to believers, " in faith, in purity, and in conversation," have been removed in the midst of their days and usefulness; " perhaps to tell us," says one, distinguished alike for his piety and talents, " that the Lord's cause does not depend on any instruments, however necessary as well as desirable they seem to us—but upon Himself, who has the residue of the Spirit."—In the last number of the British Critic, p. 242, the epithet *illustrious* is affixed to the name of Davison. Now those, who were not thoroughly acquainted with his great intellectual superiority—with his vast reach and comprehension of view—especially those who know his work on Prophecy only by hearsay, in every chapter of which there are marks of deep thought and a most powerful mind, may not perhaps consider the foregoing term as truly applicable to the subject of these hasty observations. The number, however, of his important christian virtues—and the variety of his attainments, which mark the highest order of intellect, fully sanction an epithet appropriated only to those who are

turning his eyes towards the monastic refectory[1], have as much difficulty in recognizing it, as the way-faring man in discovering a safe tread between shifting sands and *mirages;* so different an aspect has it assumed under the lapse of ages. That hall, where he held high festivals with his Prior and brethren, is now converted into a barn; and the oaken board on which he partook of his meals, changed into mangers for horses and oxen.

In the Gate-house, however, of the Priory, disfigured and deteriorated as it is, he would still discern some of the features remaining as be left them. This genuine and interesting piece of antiquity is of the perpendicular style of architecture, being erected about the same period as the greater part of the church. The front is composed of two divisions; the arch has a square head, and the spandrils are filled with quatrefoils enclosed in circular ribs; on each side are five pannels with cinquefoil heads, and pannels charged with shields: over all is a boldly projecting cornice, which runs along the front of the structure, and forms the base of the upper division. Springing from the apex of the arch, on a moulded corbel, is a highly enriched oriel window, having its angular mullions relieved with delicately carved pinnacles. On each side are eight transom-headed pannels, two of which are perforated as windows. At each angle of the front of the building is a buttress of two stages, the face of the lower one being

---

gifted with the rarest mental endowments. Indeed the appointment of *such* a character even to a Prebendal Stall, will throw a moral splendour over the administration of Lord Liverpool, whenever the disposal of his church patronage shall be discussed. But, ere long, I hope to have a fitter opportunity of paying my unbiassed tribute of respect to this most distinguished Minister of the Gospel, than is presented in the corner of a note.

[1] Refectories, or *Fratries*, were large wainscoted halls, with a crucifixion above the boards, a dresser, almories or cupboards, windows opening unto the kitchen, through which the meat was served, and desk with a bible for reading during the dinner. See Fosbrooke's Encyclopædia of Antiquities, Vol. I. p. 108.

pannelled : while at the west side we find a number of painted tiles fixed on the wall near the roof, similarly ornamented to some of those in the church. There are good reasons for believing that this Gatehouse is now not more than half of its original size, for the roof is without its corresponding parts, and the back is cased with nothing but common brick. Here, perhaps, was a chronicle composed, and the original deposited among other muniments kept under the triple keys of the Superior of the House; while some of the rooms were appropriated for the distribution of eleemosynary gifts; for it will be reckoned among the chief merits of the monastic establishments, next to their successful promotion of agriculture[1], and the estimation which is due to them as conservatories of mental treasures, that a great portion of their wealth was employed in the daily[2] exercise of acts of charity and benevolence.

[1] If their inmates did not deeply cultivate the study of divinity, we may conclude that they did well in the useful philosophy of the spade; for we are told by Mr. Turner, "that Domesday Survey gives us some indication that the cultivation of the church lands was much superior to that of any other order of society: they had much less wood upon them, and less common of pasture: and what they had appears often in small irregular pieces: while their meadow was more abundant, and in more numerous distributions." See his valuable History of the Anglo-Saxons, Vol. II. p. 167.

[2] According to that close observer of human nature, Piers Ploughman, or Robert Langland, or John Malverne, for so the author of the Vision of William has been variously styled, the dole was not dealt out so liberally to the beadsman at the gate of the abbey and priory as some of those who would wish to get rid of the system of tythes assume it to have been.

" Little had lordes to do to give lands
 from their heirs
To religions that have no ruthe
 though it rain on their aultres.
In many places there the parsons
 be themselves at ease,
Of the poor they have no pitie, and
 that is their poor charitie."

But whoever was the writer of these Visions, there is uncommon tact evinced in his

One more observation respecting the Gate-house, before we take leave of this part of our subject. It has been remarked by Dr. Johnson, in his life of Milton, that " every house in which this great man resided is historically mentioned, as if it were an injury to neglect naming any place that he honoured by his presence." In like manner may we say that this Gate-house [1] is honoured, as there is a tradition,

description of manners and character, while he has delivered what has been boldly called " prophecies of the history of the Reformation." The vehicle of allegory serves to shelter the satirist; but satirist as he was, he has imparted to many of his lines that rural and touchingly simple air which must ever continue to please. Even to the unpoetical reader, the musings on Malvern Hills, with which he opens the poem, will not be distasteful; there are many passages also full of the facetious humour of his great contemporary, Chaucer. " The Vision," remarks the great Selden, " is written in a kind of English metre which for the discovery of the infecting corruptions of those times, I prefer before many of the more seemingly serious invectives, as well for invention as for judgment." Note in Polyolbion, fol. p. 109. Hollinshed, Stow, and Wood, thus allude to this writer, who has studied so thoroughly the characters and manners of his fellow countrymen and contemporaries. " Among the learned men of that age, (Edward III.) was Robert Langland, a secular priest, born in Salopshire, in Mortimer's Clebury." Holinshed, ed. I. Vol. II. p. 1003.—" This year, John Malverne, fellow of Oriel college, in Oxford, made and finished his book entitled the Visions of Piers Plowman." Stow's Ann. p. 238.—" Robertus Langland Johannes Malverne nonnullis appellatur: fertur autem inter sui sæculi poetas maxime facetos excelluise." Wood, Hist. and Antiq. Univ. Oxon. l. ii. p. 10. 7.—And Spenser assigns to him a high poetical rank, when he says,

" Go but a lowly gate among the meaner sort,
Dare not to match thy pipe with Tityrus his style,
Nor with the Pilgrim that the Plowman plaid awhile."
*Epilogue to Shepherd's Calendar.*

[1] The following is a description of part of the Gate-house of the Priory of Bridlington, in Yorkshire, as surveyed by one of Henry the Eighth's general surveyors, and the remains of the Malvern Gate-house would encourage the opinion, that it had not been without similar accommodations; so that the King, during his temporary sejour there, would not have been without what may be called the *salon* and *boudoir* of those days. " At the cummyng yn of the said Priory is a Gate-house foure square of Towre facyon, buylded Ffrestone, and well covered with leade. And one the South Syde of the same Gate-house ys a Porter's lodge w$^t$ a Chymney, a rounde Stayre leding up to a hye Chamber wherein the thre Weks Courte ys always kepte in w$^t$ a Chymney in the same, and betweene the Stayre

which, according to Cole, represents with much probability, that Henry VII. took up his abode there—the sovereign upon whom Bacon has pronounced this noble eulogy. "His laws (whoso marks them well) were deep and not vulgar; not made on the spur of a particular occasion for the present, but out of providence for the future; to make the estate of his people still more and more happy, after the manner of the legislators in ancient and heroic times[1]."

The readers of our popular histories are imbued with the notion that the patrician class were the chief instigators with Henry to commence his work of spoliation on the ancient Church. True it is, that they shared in the division of the bounty, and many of them most largely, but those, whose knowledge is not merely superficial, are well aware that the sole suggestor and prime agent and director of this doubtful and dangerous experiment was the Secretary Cromwell. "*He*," says the accurate Strype, "had the great stroke in all this. All these counsels and methods were struck out of his head; for which, as he received the curse, and brought upon himself the hatred of many, so many more, well affected to a reformation of superstitions in the Church, extolled him highly[2];" although we question much whether these very persons would have been so desirous of pushing matters to extremity, could they have anticipated that the secularization of the monastic estates, however defensible enough in itself on Protestant principles, would have led to the plunder of bishoprics under our good virgin Queen[3].

foote and the same hie Chamber where the Courte ys kopte be tow proper Chambers one above the other w' Chymneys." Archæologia, Vol. XIX. p. 270. We are informed by Du Cange sur Joinville, Tom. II. p. 32. that the descendants of Hugh Capet held their courts in these places in imitation of the Hebrew kings.

[1] Historie of King Henry VII. Lond. 1647, p. 72.
[2] Annals of the Reformation, Vol. VI. p. 205.
[3] See Lansdowne MSS. No. 990. fol. 225. Bishop Kennett's Coll. Vol. LVI. for an

When this bold minister drew up his indictment against the monasteries, and made a condemnatory matter of it, the good Bishop Latimer petitioned that two or three religious houses in each county, and in particular that of Great Malvern, might be suffered to remain, and their estates converted to educational purposes. The letter of solicitation from this staunch champion of the Reformation to Cromwell, that Great Malvern might not be under his ban, is still extant. We shall give it to the reader in its rough black-letter language, without any attempt to modernize it, that he may see the production in all its rusticity, plainness, and strength. Now we remember to have read somewhere of a person who refused to peruse some old book because it had such very poor spelling; but we hope that this address of Latimer will not be deemed beneath notice on that account, when it is so valuable as a specimen of the idiomatic English of the age, and likewise most valuable as reflecting great credit upon Malvern Priory, seeing that its character was such as to influence a man of his apostolical purity of manners to stand forth its advocate.

"But now syre a nother thynge, that by your favour I myght be a motionare unto you, at the request of an honeste man, the Prior of Grett Malverne, in my dioc. referryng the successe of the hooll matter to your ownly approvyd wyssdoom and benyinge goodnesse in every case ffor I knoo that I doo play the ffowll, butt yett with my foolysshnesse I sumwhatt qwiett an unqwiett man, and mytygatt hys heuynesse, which I am bold to doo with you, ffor that I kno by experience your goodnesse, that you wyll bere with fowlls in there freylnesse. Thys man both heryth and feryth (as he sayth) the

account of Scambler, Bishop of Peterborough, resigning a good part of his bishopric into the *Queen's* hands. We could easily multiply instances of this kind. But this proof is sufficient for the purpose.

suppressione of hys Howse, wich thowgh he wyll be conformable in all poyntts to the kyngs hynesse plesewre and yours ons knoyn, as both I advertysed him, ande also hys bowndon dewtye ys to be, yett neurthelesse yf he thowght hys interpryesse shuld natt be mystake nor turne to ony displesewr he wold be an humble sewtere to your lordshype, and by the same to the kyngs good grace for the upstandynge of hys forsayd howse, and contynuance of the same to many good purpassesse, natt in Monkrye, he mayneth natt soo, God forbyd, butt ony other ways, as shuld be thought andeseyme good to the kyng's majestye, as to mayntayne tochynge prechynge, studye, with prayynge, ande (to the which he ys much gyvyne) good howskepynge; for to the vertu of hospitalyte he hathe byn grettly inclynyd from hys begynnynge, and ys very much commendyd in thes partees for the same : so that if ccccc. marks to the kyng's hynesse, with cc. marks to yourselffe for your good wyll might occasione the promotione of hys intentt, att leste way for the tyme of hys lyffe, he doubtyth natt to make hys freuds for the same, yf so lytull cold bringe soo much to passe. The man ys old, a good howskepere, fedyth many, and that dayly, for the contreth ys poore and full of penurye: and, alas my good Lord, shall we nat see ij. or iij. in every shyre changyd to such remydye?

"Thus too, thys honeste man is importunyte hath browght me to be younde my dewtye, savyng for the confydence and truste that I have always in your benignytye. As he hath knolege froom you, soo he wyll prepare for you, ever obedyentt to your aduertyessmentt. Syr Wylliam Kyngston can make reportt of the man.

"H. L.
"13 *Decemb.*
"*Hartl.*  Wigor[1]."

[1] The whole of this letter is given in Dugdale's Monast. Angl. N. E. p. 451. We have cited only the passages in point with our subject.

When the Priory was dissolved, it was granted by Henry, together with certain lands and tenements immediately adjoining, and others in Upton and Hanley, to William Pynnock and his heirs, who in the following year alienated the same to John Knottysford, Esq, Serjeant at Arms, from whom the Church was purchased by the inhabitants of Malvern; and to the happy circumstance of its being made parochial, we owe the preservation of a fabric so touching to the heart of the Christian, and which serves to gratify the eye of the painter as well as of the antiquary, from its having all the painter's beauties of intricacy of form, and light and shade. The older portions of the Church, the round piers worked with plain capitals, the semi-circular arches of the nave, are decidedly[1] architectural features of an early Norman origin,

[1] The following judicious hints upon the subject of Saxon and Norman edifices, we would recommend to the especial notice of certain dilettanti antiquarians, who are so oracular in their fiats as to what are, or what are not, buildings of a Saxon or of a Norman date. " On that part of our architectural history which follows the departure of the Romans from Britain, and which precedes the Norman conquest, there is of course great obscurity; but while in the days of Dr. Stukeley and Horace Walpole there appears to have been much too easy an admission of Saxon dates, on the mere appearance of the semi-circular arch, I think there has been of late perhaps too great a leaning the other way; and because we cannot directly prove that certain edifices are Saxon by documentary evidence, we have been induced too easily perhaps to consider that no Saxon buildings did exist, and have not given ourselves the trouble sufficiently to examine our earlier Norman works, to see if they were not some of them entitled to be considered as erected before the conquest. I confess I have myself been heretofore of this class of doubters as to Saxon dates; but having in various parts found buildings which are not Norman, and which from their peculiar construction cannot well be considered either as modern, or as any intermediate style, I think they must be anterior, and therefore entitled to be called Saxon." See four most instructive letters on the Ecclesiastical Architecture, by Thomas Rickman, Esq. in the twenty-fifth volume of the Archæologia, Lett. III. p. 166. These very remarks were made to us by King Leopold, when we had the honour of being his *ductor historicus* while viewing the church. This is not the place to eulogize his Majesty's taste or learning, or else, without exaggeration, we might add, that his knowledge of ecclesiastical architecture, especially of what belongs to the continental buildings called Gothic, is as accurate as that of the late Mr. Hope's on the costume of the Ancients. A *professional* architect might profit by his Majesty's judgment.

and coeval with the foundation of the monastery; the rest of the edifice is an elegant and diversified specimen of design and embellishment in the latest period of the pointed style.

Both Dugdale and Nash observe a total silence respecting the Lichfield [1] MS. which instructs us to believe, that Henry VII., his Queen, and the Princes Arthur and Henry, were so captivated with the scenery of Malvern, that the stained and painted windows in the Church, casting " a dim religious light," and constituting one of its most striking and attractive ornaments, were introduced by the devotional munificence [2] of these royal personages. Whatever uncertainty may exist as to the extent of their bounty to the Priory, we think it may be fairly and legitimately inferred, that they were in some manner, though now unknown to us, benefactors to it, from the fact, that in the large window in Jesus' Chapel, which forms the extremity of the north transept, were the figures of Henry VII. armed and crowned with an imperial crown; on his upper garments the arms of France and England; behind him, Elizabeth his queen, with the same arms on her garment; behind her, Arthur, Prince of Wales, likewise armed; behind him, Sir Reginald Bray, (which last two figures still remain perfect after 300 years), bearing in a shield argent a chevron, between three eagles' legs erased sable: behind him, Sir John Savage and Sir Thomas Lovell, all kneeling, bearing palm branches lifted up to heaven with the inscription, *Orate pro bono statu nobilissimi et excellentissimi regis Henrici Septimi et Elizabethe regine ac domini Arthuri principis filii eorundem, nec non predilectissime consortis sue et suorum trium militum* [3].

---

[1] See Chambers's History of Malvern, p. 31. for an account of this manuscript.

[2] Nash, in his Addenda, Vol. II. p. 53, says that " the painted glass in Malvern church was chiefly put here in the time of Henry VII." but he quotes no authority for this assertion.

[3] Latin terms have a *variety* of acceptations, but there cannot be a doubt, I apprehend,

28              PRIORY OF GREAT MALVERN.

Mr. Dallaway, in his Anecdotes of the Arts, has indulged in many fanciful speculations: for instance, his conjecture that the pointed arch originated from mere love of novelty, or in the caprice of the Italians [1], is unsupported by the authority of any one fact. It is, however, " passing strange," that in speaking of the interior of this church, he should have ventured peremptorily to affirm, " that all the stained glass remaining is but poorly executed," when so many compartments of the windows supply the refutation of the extravagant assertion. The rich stained glass, which admits its light into the church, in red, purple, and yellow streams, and especially from that brilliant colour the ruby, now in great measure lost, has been pronounced by connoisseurs [2] on this subject, to afford exquisite specimens,

---

that Dr. Nash is chargeable with an error in an eminent degree, when he translates *Miles* into *Esquire*. Hist. of Worcestershire, Vol. II. p. 131.—Down from Roman to what has been called kitchen Latin,—that is the Latin of the monasteries,—no instance can be produced of the word *Miles* bearing any other meaning in inscriptions than that of *Knight* or *Soldier* of Christ. The writer, in his description of the arms in the church of Great Malvern, in the time of Charles, to whom we shall have hereafter to refer, may be said to agree with every other authority on this subject when he recites, " that the last of the three attenders on theyre M^ties is S^r Thomas Lovell, a Pryvie Consellor."

" Pray for the good estate of the most noble and excellent King Henry VII. and of Elizabeth his Queen, and of the Lord Prince Arthur, their son, as well as of his most dearly beloved consort, and of their three knights." The orate pro anima was discontinued tempore Ed. VI. See Gough, Introd. p. 305. To those who are unacquainted with the Mediæval Archæology, it is fitting to remark, that the records and Latin compositions of that period universally drop the *a* in the diphthong *æ*; that is, they give regine, excellentissime, sue, &c. &c. &c. in the room of reginæ, excellentissimæ, suæ.

[1] P. 2. The tower of the Schools at Oxford is of the Italian order, and as little like true Gothic, as the Church of Great Malvern is to a Grecian temple.

[2] In his brief but well written account " of St. Mary's Church, Worcestershire," Mr. Neale, alluding to the painted and stained glass, says, " that many beautiful specimens remain:" and again, in reference to this subject, " there is still sufficient remaining to attest its original splendour." In speaking of stained glass, Mr. Rickman, in his Letters on the Ecclesiastical Architecture of France, Archæol. Vol. XXV. observes, " that a careful examination with a good telescope is (from its distance from the eye) essential to a proper

not to be surpassed by any which adorn cathedrals of the first class in this kingdom. The west window of the chapel, to which we have just alluded, consists of three divisions, all entire; and the beauty of the drawing, and the splendour of the colours, excite great admiration. Among other subjects contained in them are these; the Salutation of Elizabeth, the Visitation of the Angel to Mary, the Nativity, the Presentation in the Temple, the Blind restored to Sight, the Resurrection of Lazarus, the Multitude following our Saviour, and the Last Supper. The great east window also still glows with those gorgeous colours that modern art in vain attempts to equal, realizing all that the poet[1] has so eloquently described:—

> " As diamonded with panes of quaint device
> Innumerable of stains and splendid dyes,
> As are the tiger-moth's deep damask'd wings;
> And in the midst 'mong thousand heraldries
> And twilight saints and dim emblazonings,
> A shielded scutcheon blush'd with blood of queens and kings."

---

appreciation of its value." We have made this experiment, and therefore can vouch, (exclusive of the high authority of Mr. Rickman) that the fact is true to the letter.

[1] See the description of Agnes praying beneath the painted window, in one of the best productions of that extraordinary young man, the late John Keats, who is said by some to have fallen a victim to early studiousness; and by others, to the poisoned arrows of criticism. That he was "cursed with too much sensibility," is sufficiently obvious, from the following passage in the Preface to his Endymion:—" This may be speaking too presumptuously, and may deserve a punishment, but no feeling man will be forward to inflict it: he may leave me alone, with the conviction that there is no fiercer hell than the failure in a great object." His fate may be likened to that of

> " A bud bit by an envious worm
> Ere it could spread its sweet leaves to the air,
> Or dedicate its beauty to the sun."

Dwelling, in the true spirit of criticism, more upon the beauties than the defects of this youthful genius, we shall say, at the hazard of forfeiting all pretensions to nicety of discrimination, that there are many passages in his Isabella, the Eve of St. Agnes, and in

By a benefaction from the late Princess Charlotte of Wales, the west window in like manner has been filled with splendid representations of Pontiffs, Prelates, and Saints, brought from less observable situations in other parts of the church.

Among the Harleian MSS.[1] is an account, written in the time of Charles I. of the arms in the church of Great Malvern. The following quotations from it will not only be acceptable to the mere antiquary, but from their plaintive moralizing tone leave a pleasing impression upon the minds of those, who relish the simple reflections and phraseology of the earlier annalists, and which are in such *strict keeping*, as the painters call it, with their subject; while the pompous inscriptions, which sometimes accompany royal shields, have in them the sting of an epigram, since they oftener show what they whom they commemorate ought to have been, than what they actually were. "Let no man deceive you with vain words," is the admonition of an apostle, which the sage or the moralist will apply to those who seek to blazon forth a name to the world, which wisdom had consigned to oblivion: for how many, canopied in state, have been such idolaters of vain glory, or oppressors of their species, that bursts of scorn or indignation escape at the very sight of their proud monuments.

After alluding to the representation of Prince Arthur, "nypt in the bud w[th] an untymely deathe, so that he hasted fyrst who by nature's course shoulde have gon last," our genealogist thus proceeds: "Lastly I conclude w[th] the large west windowe, representinge to vs the dreadfull daye of Judgment wheare on the ryght hand is Quarterly Fraunce and England, supported w[th] towe hoares, Argent, and couered

his noble fragment of Hyperion, which render him fully deserving "laureâ donandus Apollinari," of the sacred name of poet, and therefore justly entitled to a niche in the temple of Fame.

[1] No. 2205. fo. 17—19. Armes in the Churche of Great Malvern.

w^th a Duke's crowne, Or. The Duke's crowne shewethe hee was yet a subiect, although these Armes w^thout difference threaten that hee aymethe at a kingdome, w^ch he cruelly won, and drowned hys singular wysdome, renowned valure, and other rare partes, in a blouddy vsurpation. O Richard the thyrd, haddest thou deepely consydered of the Judgment seate (the resemblance wheareof by all lykelihood thy bounty here erected), thou wouldest never so highely have prysed a puffe of ambition. On the other syde are the Armes of hys Duches, afterwardes Queen disorderly marshalled and thus quartered. 1. Gules a fesse between six crosses croslets Or. 2. Or. three cheuerons Gules. 3. Quarterly Argent and Gules fretted Or a bendelet Sables. 4. Checkic Or and Asure a cheueron Erm. Impalinge Gules a Salteyre Argent couered w^th her husbandes, and supported w^th towe beares Argent. So Royalty beginnethe and endethe the Armory of this Charge[1]."

If rareness heighten the interest of that which in itself is interesting, either as an object of taste or of high antiquity, then the carved stone image in the recess of Jesus' Chapel claims particular notice. Stukeley[2] described it to be a knight covered with a mail and his surcoat: in his right hand a halbert like a pickaxe; in his left, a round target. Gough[3] says, this figure is in the oldest mail armour; and Carter[4]

[1] This remarkable coat of arms is still in existence, and is now to be found in the third window on the south side of the nave. The following opinion is given by Nash, on the authority of George Lord Lyttleton. "The two shields, containing the arms and supporters of Richard III. and the other those of his queen, have both coronets over them, which, perhaps, is the earliest instance of coronets borne over the arms of princes and nobility as at this day." Addenda, vol. ii. p. 53. The late Lord Colchester first pointed out these arms to us; and he observed at the same time, that it cost him a good hour's work before he could discover them, in consequence of their having been completely misplaced by an ignorant glazier.

[2] Itinerarium curiosum.
[3] Sepulchral Monuments in Great Britain.
[4] Ancient sculpture and painting.

states, that no similar figure ever came under his observation. Upon the principle just referred to, the yellow or orange-coloured tiles in the pavement of this church are not to be overlooked; they are finely glazed, and richly ornamented; many with armorial bearings: those of the woman-hearted Confessor [1], of Henry VII. (France and England quarterly [2]) of the Abbey of Westminster, and of several great baronial families. But as a more specific mention may be desiderated by those who are versed in the science of heraldry, the following then will, perhaps, be interesting to persons of such tastes.

"1. A cross moline inter 5 martlets for y$^e$ Abbey of Westminster to w$^{ch}$ this Priory belonged.

2. Three Lions passant gardant for England, or King Henry y$^e$ 3$^d$ who was a great Benefactor.

---

[1] "The woman-hearted Confessor prepares
The evanescence of the Saxon line."
*Eccles. Sketches*, p. 33.

But we should be disposed to dispute the accuracy of this epithet, if meant to refer to all the actions of this last legitimate Anglo-Saxon king. In the bestowal of his ecclesiastical preferments, there was nothing timid or vacillating in his conduct. He treated the authority of the Pope with the same bold disregard as Martin Luther himself would have done, if invested with similar powers and functions. "When Edward the Confessor," says Sir Francis Palgrave, "notified the promotion of a prelate, it was by the promulgation of a charter, which stated, that he had given and granted the bishopric, and all that thereto belonged. Not the slightest allusion is made to the will of the Pontiff, or the postulation of the Clergy: he declares his will and pleasure, and in terms more than emulating those employed by our eighth Henry in the plenitude of his power. The same royal authority controlled the other branches of ecclesiastical promotion. The abbot was elected by the king's consent; he resigned his monastery in favour of a successor, by the king's license; and when the Bishop wished to remove his See, he applied in the first instance, not to the Pope, but to the King." The Rise and Progress of the English Commonwealth, Part I. p. 173, 174.

[2] "The first instance extant of an approach to the system of quartering arms, which," says Sir Nicholas Harris Nicholas, "was not regularly adopted in this country until the reign of Edward III. is afforded in the Bohuns." See Remarks on the Seals attached to the Letter from the Barons of England to Pope Boniface the Eighth. Archæologia, Vol. XXI. p. 192.

3. A Bend cotised inter 6 Lions rampant, for Bohun Earl of Hereford.

4. Barry of 6 on a Chief, 2 Pallets inter 2 Esquires, an Escocheon of Pretence Ermine for Mortimer Earl of March.

5. Quarterly on f. $2^d$ and $3^d$ a Fret. over all a Bend for Spencer Earl of Glocester.

6. A Fess inter 6 Martlets for Beauchamp[1] of Powike.

7. 3. Cheuronels for Clare Earl of Glocester.

8. A Fess inter 6 crosses botony for Beauchamp Earl of Warwic.

The same arms are on y$^e$ Floor in divers parts of y$^e$ Church. Checquy a Cheuron, and y$^e$ arms of Bracy, viz. : a Fess and 2 Mullets in Chief: with this Date all behind y$^e$ Altar after y$^e$ aforesaid 8 Coats.

There have been some, and those professed antiquaries too, whose notions on these tiles are certainly of a most original nature, conceiving them to be *Alhambra* tiles, brought from Portugal, although there is such clear and decisive evidence of their having been manufactured in Britain. Now the least learned antiquary is aware, that after heraldic devices were carved or painted upon escutcheons, or stained in glass in consecrated places, they were painted upon glazed bricks and tiles on the floors. During the middle centuries, most of the great Abbeys and Priories had kilns for preparing them, from which also the conventual churches were supplied. The most obvious and rational conclusion therefore is, that the monks, having acquired this branch of encaustic painting, devoted much of their leisure time to it. At first these tiles, baked almost to vitrification, and admirably calculated to resist damp and wear, were of an irregular shape, but afterwards they were made equilateral, and about four inches square; " and when

---

[1] De Bello-Campo, as it is written in some charters and other public instruments.

arranged and connected," observes Mr. Fosbrooke[1], " produced an effect very much resembling the Roman designs, yet wanting their simplicity and taste. There will be, however, with the most sceptical, a perfectly satisfactory settlement of the question as to their being of foreign fabrication, when they learn, that within the last year a kiln[2] has been discovered on the Priory farm, in which were found tiles of the same dimensions and materials as those that decorate the floors of the church. On one of these tiles, which is fixed in the third pillar on the north side of the nave, we have an inscription, which, for its curiosity, is well worthy to be recorded; and, when translated into intelligible English, will read thus :—

Thenke . mon . þi . liffe .
mai . not . eu . endure .
þat . þow . dost. þi. self.
of . þat . þow . art . surve .
but . þat . þow . gebest .
un . to . þi . sectur . cure .
and . eu . hit . abaile . þe .
hit . is . but . abenture .

Think man thy life
May not ever endure
That thou dost thyself
Of that thou art sure
But that thou givest
To thy executors cure
An ever it avail thee
It is but a venture[3].

---

[1] Encyclop. of Antiq. Vol. I. p. 104.
[2] See Note D. Appendix.
[3] A tile with the same inscription as that just mentioned was dug up in the ruins of an old house called the Ranger's Lodge, now the property of Lady Lyttleton. In alluding again to this venerable person, for whether referring to her virtues or her years, the epithet *venerable* is strictly applicable, as her Ladyship has now attained the honoured old age of

The spectator of antiquarian taste will examine with attention a small chapel in the aisle of the church, the vaulting of which is decorated with fan tracery, and other analogous enrichments. The exterior of this chapel, or perhaps it was nothing more than a recess occupied by an ancient tomb, at all events it is quite erroneous to style it, as some have done, a Confessional[1], is pannelled with quatrefoils, over which is a cornice with figures bearing shields. His eye, after surveying a screen of beautifully carved oak on the left side of the chancel, will also notice the range of antique stalls, the subsellæ of which exhibit various grotesque and other carvings in *alto relievo*. Among the subjects are to be seen a miser on his death-bed, with the priest at his head, and a leach at his feet, to whom he is offering his money bags; 2. the prodigal son; 3. a small figure holding a large goblet in each hand, designed, no doubt, for an emblem of gluttony, as he is

---

ninety-one, we cannot refrain from saying that her coronet well deserves to be entwined with the wreath of public gratitude : indeed, her benevolent feelings, like the genius of some great men, may be said to burn brightest at the last. Without specifying the numerous charities elsewhere bestowed by this ornament of her sex, for of them we have a perfect knowledge, suffice it to observe, that in this parish, and within a few years, her Ladyship has made extensive additions to the Sunday school, erected at her sole expence—contributed largely to the school of industry—to the infant school, of both of which she was the establisher, besides being a most liberal benefactress to the North-hill Royal school, and other institutions of this place. And all these things " that are excellent, lovely in conduct, and of good report," have been done by this admirable woman out of an income which many in the station of life to which she belongs would deem inadequate for its due maintenance. Truly then, may we exclaim, in the words of the great Father of English poetry, " she will be holden digne of reverence." Who indeed can fail to be struck with the image of such excellence ?

[1] Directly opposite to this description of a Confessional, is that which has been called so in this church. " On each side of the altar at Crewkerne, in Somersetshire, is a door leading into a small room; that by which the penitent entered for confession has two swine carved over it, to signify their pollution: that by which they returned, two angels, to signify their purity. At Gloucester, the Confessional is a large chair by the side of the door." Fosbrooke's Encyclopædia of Antiquities, Vol. I. p. 97.

sitting over the fragments of a repast; 4. three rats strangling a cat.

Swift, in one of his cutting sarcasms, called our churches the *dormitories of the living*. The *Miserere* was a very ingenious expedient of the Priors for preventing theirs from becoming so. It was indeed as admirable a contrivance against the indulgence of fits of somnolency, as the American camp meetings are for keeping alive the excitement of fanatical passions. Dr. Milner has thus accurately described this monitor to drowsy monks:—" The small shelving stool, which the seats of the stalls formed, when turned up in their proper position, is called a *Miserere*. On these, the monks and canons of ancient times, with the assistance of their elbows on the upper part of the stalls, half supported themselves during certain parts of their long offices, not to be obliged always to stand or kneel. The stool, however, was so contrived, that if the body became supine by sleep, it naturally fell down, and the person who rested upon it was thrown forward into the middle of the choir. The present usage in this country is to keep them always turned down, in which position they form a firm horizontal seat; an indulgence that was very rarely granted to those who kept choir in ancient times [1]."

[1] Historical Account of Winchester Cathedral, Note, p. 60. If the reports of the Commissioners at the General Visitation of the Monasteries were not extant to assure us that so many brotherhoods had completely debased themselves in sensual indulgence, we should have doubted, from the severe daily discipline with which they were fenced in, that human nature could have fallen into such corruption. The following regulations, if strictly enforced, were surely calculated to restrain the monks, since a rigorous employment of time has always been considered as the best security against the practice of every species of wickedness. Matins, or Matutina, or Lands, from midnight until Prime. The morning service commenced about three A. M., and was called Matins, or Lauds. Prime, or Prima; from about six A. M. Tierce, this service immediately succeeded Matins. " If the office of Lauds be finished by daybreak as is fit, let them begin Prime; if not let them wait for daylight. Tierce, or Tertia, from about nine A. M. to Sext. Sext, or

Confining ourselves to the illustration of the antiquities of the church, we shall pass over in silence its modern monuments and inscriptions. On a very handsome monument of alabaster, on the steps, by the south side of the altar, and standing on a sort of chapel beneath it, are the figures of John Knottesford, Esq., and Jane, his lady, in recumbent postures. He is represented, in plate armour, on the altar monument; several children are at their sides. Against the east arch at their feet, on a piece of marble, are these arms, viz. S on a cross engrailed A a mullet for Knottesford, impaling O. 2 Pallets G for Knightly. Under them is this inscription: " Here lieth the body of John Knottesford, Esquire, servant to King Henry the Eighth, and Jane his wife, daughter to Sir Richard Knightly, who being first named to Mr. William Lumley, had issue John Lord Lumley, and by John Knottesford had issue five daughters and coheirs: he dyed in the year 1589." At the head of the tomb is a large figure of a lady kneeling before a desk, and looking towards the altar, with these arms on the desk, viz. A. 6 lions rampant, S for Savage impales Knottesford, being the eldest daughter Anne, who caused this monument to be erected.

The remains of many of the ancient family of Lygon[1] in this

Sexta, from about twelve, or noon, to Nones. Nones, or Nona, from about two or three P. M. to Vespers. Vespers, or Vespera, from about four o'clock to Complin, or second Vespers. Completorium, or Compline, Second Vespers, about seven o'clock." See Chronology of History, by Sir Harris Nicholas, p. 184.

[1] See MS. account of Worcestershire families *sub nomine*, in Biblioth. Societ. Antiq. also Genealogy of the Beauchamp Family in Genealogical History of the Crooke Family, by Sir Alexander Croke, D.C.L. Oxon. 1832, Vol. III. p. 140: and that of Dr. Nash previous to the Lygon connexion with the baronial family of Beauchamp of Powyke, Hist. of Worc. Vol. II. p. 264. We are told by this last writer, that the Lygons had a right to quarter twenty-seven coats of arms, Vol. II. p. 117. After this minute observation, it is extraordinary, that in his account of the parish of Mamble or Mamele, and enumeration of the lords of the soil, he should, if acquainted with the fact, have omitted

county have here found their resting places. The inscriptions over them chiefly commemorate their household virtues, domestic affections, and social charities. But in reading the simple and affecting lines affixed to the stone which records the death of Maria, wife of William Lygon of Madresfield, we feel that we are treading on the ashes of her, who was not beautiful only, but united with transient beauty the more durable gifts of piety and virtue.

> " Stay, passenger, and from this dusty urne
> Both what I was and what thou must be learne.
> Grace, virtue, beauty, had no privilege
> That everlasting statute to abridge,
> That all must die ; then, gentle friend, with care
> In life for death and happiness prepare."

---

> " Hark—speaking to themselves
> Are Malvern sweet nine bells ;
> Now they troll—troll—troll [1]."

Thus blithely is supposed to have sung a poetical pastor of Malvern, whose lays on another subject we shall give as an appropriate conclusion to our Dissertation. But where are the other three? (for six only now remain,) is the first and natural question of the lover of campanology. Gone, irrecoverably gone, to St. Mary Overy's church in Southwark, is the sorrowing reply. Through whose instrumentality, or for what price, or upon what occasion—on these points we are unhappily without the irresistible evidence of dates, figures, or

to notice that *Henry Lyggon* received the manor of Mamele in the reign of Henry the Fourth. For this statement see the learned work just referred to, Vol. II. Book III. Chap. I.

[1] For a further reference to the supposed author of these lines " of rude and homely vulgar poesie," see Note at the end of our Dissertation.

facts. When Cole was at Malvern, in 1746, the Parish Clerk told him[1] that they had been sold some fifty or sixty years ago. This great antiquary, however, seems, from some subsequent remarks which he makes on this subject, to have been as incredulous respecting the truth of this statement, as he would be upon that of an old legend.

But if it be a sad truth to learn that a grand act of larceny has been committed on three bells, it would have been still sadder if the tenor bell had been removed, as it is the most musical and the most ancient of them all, bearing the following inscription, in what appears to be the Lombardic[2] character, since it exactly resembles the motto on the earliest seal of the city of Norwich[3], which is assigned by most of our eminent antiquarians to that origin.

## VIRGINIS: EGREGIE: VOCOR: CAMPANA: MARIE*[4]

The antiquity of this bell may be startling to some of our readers, who are not aware that bells were used in the time of the Anglo-Saxons. If our assertion be not sufficient, the following passage from the venerable Bede will, it is hoped, satisfy the most sceptical on this point. "She, while tarrying at that time in the Sisters' Dormitory, suddenly heard in the air the well known sound of a bell, whereby,

---

[1] MSS. Brit. Mus. Vol. X. fol. 119.

[2] "The Lombardic running-hand was a branch of the Roman, modelled after that used in the sixth and seventh centuries. There is a striking resemblance between the Lombardic and *Merovingian* running-hands. Lombardic characters are still to be seen in some charters of the thirteenth century, even in Germany. The affinity between the Roman, Lombardic, and Merovingian running-hand is so great that they may be considered as one." Encyclopædia of Antiquities, Vol. I. p. 484.

[3] See Archæologia, Vol. XXI. p. 80.

[4] Decyphered in Roman characters, this inscription stands thus: "Virginis egregiæ vocor campana Mariæ."—i. e. "I am called the Virgin Mary's Bell."

when any one had been called from this life, they were wont to be roused or summoned to prayers[1]."

Malvern Church, indeed, seems fated to experience every sort of spoliation. Its very porch has fallen into lay hands; and its roof would not now have been crumbling into ruins, had not the lead been stolen. Its exterior truly may be compared to those cabinets of ivory one sometimes meets with in old family mansions, scratched, flawed, splintered, carrying all the marks of time-worn decay. "Albeit, however unused to the *sanguine* mood," we cannot quite despair that public piety and liberality will preserve an Edifice which is connected with so many associations of the historical kind, and which calls up so many sentiments delightful to minds of pure taste and religious sensibility. We trust then, that the hope is not presumptuous, especially after the example of the Illustrious Personage[2] to whom these pages are inscribed,—an example which has such various and noble claims to respect and imitation, that those of the upper classes of the Laity, as well as of the Clergy, who have resorted to Malvern for the renovation of their health, and not in vain—will do something—will do a little—will do all they can to save the exterior from further dilapidation; now that our humble efforts, may we be permitted to add without incurring the risk of being taxed with the fault of egotism, have been crowned with complete success, in repairing the interior. That this assistance is not craved before it is peeniliarly needed, the Extract in the Appendix, from a Report given of

---

[1] " Hæc tunc in dormitorio sororum pausans audivit subito in aere *notum* companæ *sonum*, quo ad orationes excitari vel convocari solebant cum quis de sæculo fuisset evocatus." Hist. Eccles. Gentis Angl. Lib. IV. Cap. XXIII.

[2] The Duchess of Kent marked the Church for an object of her beneficent liberality, soon after her arrival at Malvern. Her Royal Highness's donation of £50. was immediately followed by a similar sum from King Leopold.

the state of the Church, at a general meeting of the parishioners, in 1831, will bring before them evidence broad and undeniable as the light of day. At a time when there are those who impiously desire to signalize themselves by pulling down churches,—let us trust that this disgraceful fact will so rouse the holy zeal of every true lover of God and man, and more especially of those who are dedicated to the service of the Church,—will so animate them, that they make no delay in preserving those ancient places of divine worship which are still left to us.

Eighty-three years ago, the following remark was made by that distinguished ornament of our Church, Bishop Butler:—" In the present turn of the age, one may observe a wonderful frugality in every thing that has respect to religion, and extravagance in every thing else. But amidst the appearance of opulence and improvement in all common things which are now seen in most places, it would be hard to find a reason why these monuments of *ancient piety* should not be preserved in their original beauty and magnificence[1]." Some there are who think, that symptoms of this disposition are appearing in the present time: speaking for ourselves, we cannot imagine the return of that day of *Vandalism and Fanaticism*, when Christian men of this country shall become supinely negligent of upholding and adorning their terrestrial sanctuaries, before they pass into their Maker's temple of the heavens. Horace told the Roman people, that

" Dii multa neglecti dederunt
Hesperiæ mala luctuosæ,"

and predicted, that their misfortunes would not terminate, till they had repaired the fanes of the gods :—

[1] See Primary Charge to the Clergy of Durham, A. D. 1751.

> " Delicta majorum immeritus lues,
> Romane, donec templa refeceris
> Ædesque labentes deorum et
> Fœda nigro simulacra fumo."

And if this Protestant nation shall ever become settled into a profound indifference respecting the fate of its fabrics consecrated to the purposes of religion, it will, we fear, cease to be the favoured country for the diffusion of the triumphs of truth; and instead of being thus exalted above all the kingdoms of the earth, it will lose the protection of heaven, because no longer deserving it. For where is the people, we would ask, with whom the Giver of all Good has dealt as he has dealt with us? But if that prophecy is no longer to receive its accomplishment, which proclaims, that " Kings and Queens shall be the nursing fathers and mothers" of our Church, adieu to the magnificence of this nation's destinies —the beauty and strength of our Israel are gone—never to rise again.

David calls the house of God, " the beauty of holiness." Yet there are some of such perverted taste and feeling, as to deem no place holy which is beautiful; while again we meet with others who are fully persuaded that to bestow much cost and care upon any ancient religious edifices of a cathedral character, " partakes," to use the words of Sir Walter Raleigh " of a kind of popery, and proceeds from an idolatrous disposition." To such as may labour under this mean and fanciful apprehension, we would respond in the exclamation of the great Chillingworth : " What, if out of devotion towards God, out of a desire that he should be worshipped, as in spirit and truth in the first place, so all in the beauty of holiness—what, if out of fear that too much simplicity and nakedness in the public service of God, may beget in the ordinary sort of men dull and stupid irreverence, and out of hope that the outward state and glory of it being well disposed and wisely moderated, may engender, quicken, increase, and nourish the inward reverence, respect, and devotion which is due unto God's sovereign majesty and power—I say, what if out of these considerations, the governors of our Church, more of late than formerly, have set themselves to adorn and beautify the places where God's honour dwells, and to make them as heaven-like as they can with earthly ornaments—is this a sign that they are warping towards popery? Is their devotion in the Church of England an argument that she is coming over to the Church of Rome?"

Now even a Bolingbroke would not be thought a stranger to those hallowed emotions which are elicited " by the solemn magnificence of a well ornamented church[1]." Can their zeal then be questioned on the subject, whose religion is not a transient impulse, but a permanent principle, producing an uninterrupted series of useful exertions? Can we entertain the suspicion for a moment that *they* will not put forth their influence to restore the exterior of the venerable church of Great Malvern to its pristine state of beauty and magnificence? No—we feel confident, that such will answer as willingly to our simple but Christian appeal as a band of faithful warriors would to the trumpet-call, which summons them to preserve their honour, their freedom, and their loyalty.

It will not be straying materially from the subject of this Dissertation, to close it with an old Song, the date of which composition, whether written in the reign of James the First, or at a later period, has baffled the researches of the most persevering antiquarians[2]. The

---

[1] See Philosophical Essays, Vol. II. p. 324.

[2] " One copy," says Nash, " was found dated 1600, but on what authority I know not." Hist. of Worc. Vol. II. p. 127. We have seen an old common-place book of the

worthy rhymer will certainly not take his place among the Immortals of this earth, as they are called, for not a single trace of the higher poetry of his betters, is discoverable in this production, but still we are indebted to him for his quaint memorial lines, since they are authority for the interesting fact, that Great Malvern was as famous in by-gone days, as it now is, for the salubrity of its air, and the medicinal properties of its waters.

> " As I did walk alone,
>    Late in an evening,
> I heard the voice of one
>    Most sweetly singing;
> Which did delight me much,
> Because the song was such,
> And ended with a touch,
>    O praise the Lord.

> " The God of sea and land,
>    That rules above us,
> Stays his avenging hand,
>    'Cause he doth love us;
> And doth his blessings send,
> Altho' we do offend,
> Then let us all amend,
>    And praise the Lord.

---

Rev. John Webb, in which it is said that Edmund Rea, who was Vicar of Great Malvern, in 1610, was the author of this song, and of the metrical fragment quoted a few pages before, though we desire not to be understood as contending for the positive certainty of this assertion. Webb was incumbent in 1708. " He gave," says Cole, " 100$^{pds}$ in order to get the Queen's Bounty toward the augmentation of the Vicarage, which is about 55 per añn." MSS. Vol XXV. fol. 194. The reader will bear in mind that this was written in 1746. The date of Cole's Letter to his friend Walpole respecting " the inexactitude of Tom Hearne," was September 30, 1780.

> " Great Malvern on a rock,
>   Thou standest surely;
> Do not thyself forget,
>   Living securely;
> Thou hast of blessings store—
> No country town hath more—
> Do not forget therefore,
>   To praise the Lord.
>
> " Thou hast a famous church,
>   And rarely builded;
> No country town[1] hath such,
>   Most men have yielded;
> For pillars stout and strong,
> And windows large and long,
> Remember in thy song,
>   To praise the Lord.

---

[1] The lady who, in our hearing, desired a rustic of Malvern not to call it a *town*, as she did not wish to be reminded of gas-lights, flag pavements, and noisy streets, will consider our Poet as sinning most egregiously against all propriety in here using the word "town." That others may not suppose he has committed a great blunder, and violated all historical truth, we will cite, for their instruction, the following passage from a writer who appears to have investigated the subject in all its bearings. " We imagine that a town, according to the import of its name, must consist of houses, built side by side, and standing in rows, streets, or lanes. But the primeval town was a tract of land enjoyed by a community; and it mattered little whether the dwellings were placed side by side, or disposed up and down the township. Nay, a town may be a very good town, according to the old law, though not a house remains standing. It is equally erroneous to consider, with Hume, that trade formed the characteristic of the burgess. He may have cheapened and chaffered, and bought and sold; but in his primitive occupation he was a tiller of land, for it was the land, the burgage, which gave him his qualification. In Ireland, the word *town* retains its real sense; and as Miss Edgeworth informs us, English visitors are often perplexed by its application, and it was probably in use among the Belgic Britons before the Saxon invasion. *Ton*, in the ancient British language, is still applied to a large tract of pasture lantl." Edinburgh Review, Vol. XXXVI. p. 311. Sir Francis Palgrave, in his Analysis of the Anglo-Saxon State, observes, " the first and primary element appears to be the community, which in England during the Saxon period, was denominated the *town* or *township*; (*tun*, from *tynan*, to enclose*,* ibid.) In times comparatively modern, this term has become less frequently used, and has been often superseded by the word *manor*." The Rise and Progress of the English Commonwealth, Part I. p. 65.

" There is God's service read,
　　With reverence duly;
There is his word preached,
　　Learned and truly;
And ev'ry Sabbath day,
Singing of psalms, they say,
'Tis surely the only way,
　　　　To praise the Lord.

" The Sun in glory great,
　　When first it riseth,
Doth bless thy happy seat,
　　And thee adviseth;
That then it's time to pray,
That God may bless thy way,
And keep thee all the day,
　　　　To praise the Lord.

" That thy prospect's good,
　　None can deny thee;
Thou hast great store of wood,
　　Growing hard by thee,
Which is a blessing great,
To roast and boil thy meat,
And thee in cold to heat,
　　　　O praise the Lord.

" Preserve it, I advise,
　　Whilst that thou hast it;
Spare not, in any wise,
　　But do not waste it,
Lest thou repent too late,
Remember Hanley's[1] fate,
In time shut up thy gate,
　　　　And praise the Lord.

---

[1] It is supposed by some " that Hanley's fate" has reference to Richard, the great Earl of Warwick and Salisbury, who obtained possession of this Castle by marriage, as we are told by Nash, vol. i. p. 557, but he being attainted of high treason, his estates were escheated to the Crown.

" A chace for royal deer,
    Round doth beset thee ;
For many I do fear,
    For aught they get thee ;
Yet, tho' they eat away
Thy corn ; thy grass, and hay ;
Do not forget, I say,
        To praise the Lord.

" That noble chace doth give
    Thy beasts their feeding,
Where they in summer live,
    With little heeding ;
Thy sheep and swine there go,
So doth thy horse also,
'Till winter brings in snow,
        Then praise the Lord.

" Turn up thine eyes on high,
    There fairly standing,
See Malvern's highest hill,
    All hills commanding ;
They all confess at will
Their sov'reign, Malvern Hill,
Let it be mighty still,
        And praise the Lord.

" When western winds do rock,
    Both town and country ;
Thy hill doth break the shock,
    They cannot hurt thee ;
When waters great abound,
And many a country's drown'd,
Thou standest safe and sound ;
        O praise the Lord.

" Out of that famous hill,
    There daily springeth,
A water passing still,
    Which always bringeth,
Great comfort to all them,
That are diseas'd men,
And makes them well again,
        To praise the Lord.

"　Hast thou a wound to heal,
　　The which doth grieve thee;
　Come then unto this well,
　　It will relieve thee;
　*Noli me tang*ere,
　And other maladies,
　Have here their remedies—
　　　　Prais'd be the Lord.

"　To drink thy water's store,
　　Lie in thy bushes,
　Many with ulcers sore,
　　Many with bruises,
　Who succour find from ill,
　By money given still—
　Thanks to the Christian will,
　　　　O praise the Lord.

"　A thousand bottles there
　　Were filled weekly,
　And many costrils rare,
　　For stomachs sickly;
　Some of them into Kent;
　Some were to London sent;
　Others to Berwick went—
　　　　O praise the Lord."

# APPENDIX.

# APPENDIX.

### Note A.

"Aldwinus erat quidam ab eo factus Monachus sicque in vastissimo illo saltu quod Malvernum vocatur Eremiticam vitam cum Guidone socio exercebat. Guidoni post longos agones compendiosius ad gloriam visum, vt Ierosolymam iret, vbi labore itinerario vel Domini sepulcrum videret, vel fœliciter manu Sarracenorum mortem anticiparet. Aldwinus, eidem sententiæ inductus, consilium tamen cum patre Wilstano quæsiuit. Dissuasit Pontifex, et ardentem refrigerauit, dicens: 'Noli sodes Aldwine quoquàm ire, sed in loco mane: crede mihi, miraberis si scires quod scio: quantum in illo loco per te Deus operaturus est.' Discessit hoc audito Monachus, firmoque iam durabat in proposito, leuabatque spe prophetiæ omne genus erumnæ. Nec multò pòst vaticinium properauit impleri:—veniebantque ad Aldwinum alter post unum,—tertius post alterum, et ita vsque ad *tricenarium*[1] numerum: affluebatque eis in primis victualium copia, vicinis beatos se iudicantibus, qui aliquid Dei famulis impertirentur. Quod verò eis deerat, fide supplebant, dum parvi facerent, si carerent carnali cibo, qui spirituali pinguescebant gaudio."—Saville's Scriptores, fol. Lond. 1596. Gul. Malmesb. de gestis Pontificum Angl. Lib. iii. fol. 160.

### Note B.

"Sewlfus quidam negociator ad eum quotannis venire consueuerat, vt ejus consilio morbis mederetur animæ. Cui semel post absolutionem factam dixit, Sæpe peccata, quæ confessus es, reiteras, quia (vt dicitur) opportunitas latronem

[1] The following Note should have been inserted in the body of the work. Due praise is to be given to Nash as a diligent collector of what others have written on the antiquities of his county; but he is often most careless in his quotations. By a stroke of his magical pen, thirty eremites are here turned into three hundred. As there were no political economists—no Professors Malthus's in those days, to point out the evils incident to a redundant population, a community of three hundred taking possession of an uncultivated tract of land, might have increased the danger of perishing by starvation, or the diseases which not unfrequently result from insufficient diet.

facit. Quare consulo vt Monachus fias: quod si feceris, horum peccatorum opportunitate carebis. Cùm retulisset ille, non se monachum pro rigore propositi fieri posse. Substomachatus Episcopus, Vade (inquit), Monachus fies, velis nolis; sed cùm vitiorum vtensilia in te senuerint. Quod nos posteà vidimus; quia in nostro Monasterio, iam senectute fractus, morbo admonente conuersus est. Sed licèt multotiens pœnituerit, quotiescunque tamen dictum Episcopi aliquis præsentasset ei, reuocabat impetum, remolliebat animum."—Gul. Malmesb. de gestis Pontificum Angl. Lib. iii. fol. 160.

## Note C.

"Sed quia Fuldense cœnobium nominaui, dicam quod ibidem accidisse vir reuerendus mihi narrauit, Walkerius, Prior Maluerniæ, cuius verbis qui non credit iniuriam religioni facit. Non (ait) plusquā quindecim anni sunt, quòd in eodem loco exitialis lues grassata, priùs Abbatem corripuit, mox multos Monachorū extinxit; superstites primò quisq̨ sibi timere, orationes et eleemosynas largiores facere; sed processu temporis, vt est omnium hominum natura pedetentim metu dempto omittere; Cellerarius præsertim qui palàm et ridiculè clamitaret, non posse penum tot expensis sufficere; sperasse se nuper aliquod alleuiamentum, pro tot elationibus funerum: nihil ultrà spei esse, si quod viui nequissent mortui consumerent. Itaque cùm quadam nocte propter necessaria soporem distulisset diu, tandem elaqueatis morarum retibus in dormitorium ire pergebat; et ecce rem miram auditurus es: videt in capitulo Abbatem, et omnes, qui obierant illo anno, eo quo excesserant ordine sedere: timidus et effugere gestiens, vi retractus est; increpitus et Monastico more flagellis exercitus, audiuit verba Abbatis in hanc omnino sententiam, Stultum esse de alterius morte emolumento inhiare, cùm sors cuiusque sub eodem pendeat fato. Impium esse cum Monachus omnem vitam in Ecclesiæ consumpserit obsequio, vt careat saltem vnius anni post mortem stipendio: Illum citissimè obiturum, sed quicquid pro eo fieret ad aliorum, quibus abstulerat, refundendum commodum, iret modò et alios corrigeret exemplo, quos corruperat verbo. Abijt ille, et nihil se vanum vidisse tam recentibus plagis, quàm proximo sui obitu monstrauit."—Willielmi Malmesburiensis de gestis Regum Anglorum [de Willielmi primo, Lib. iii.] p. 65. edit. Lond. 1596.

## Note D.

The following remarks are the result of an investigation on this subject by Mr. Eginton, a young architect of much promise, and a devoted admirer of buildings

APPENDIX. 53

after the Gothic manner. The paper was drawn up at my request; and with it Mr. E. has obligingly prepared a drawing as a suitable accompaniment to his interesting observations.

"The tile-kiln was discovered seven feet under ground, on land formerly belonging to the Priory of Malvern, and carefully opened in the presence of Dr. Card, and several other gentlemen interested in the study of antiquities. A correct idea of it is formed from the accompanying section, its length being 35 feet.

A ROMAN TILE-KILN, as found by HARVEY EGINTON, ARCHITECT

"The arch most exposed to heat was composed of brick, and the outer arch of common red tiles. The sides were carefully backed in with Malvern rag-stone, evidently to prevent the kiln bursting from the intense heat; and the equal necessity of protecting the crown of the arch probably suggested the idea of burying the kiln. The floor, on which there can be no doubt the tiles were burnt, was ingeniously constructed with bricks, the outside ones being worked into the wall at the springing of the arch, the ends of which being bevelled, the middle brick acted as a key-stone; a peculiarity in this floor was its remaining unvitrified, although the whole of the bricks in the arch, and even the tiles of the outer arch,

I

were perfectly glazed. The floor on which the fire was placed being the natural soil (marl), was burnt till in hardness and colour it resembled lime-stone. As no apertures were discovered for the escape of smoke, and as a quantity of charcoal was found near it, it is probable the tiles discovered were similar to those in the Churches of Great and Little Malvern, but these differ in external appearance from most that I have seen, in the characters, or pattern upon them. In most instances the pattern is sunk in the body of the tile; in these it is painted upon the *surface*. It may therefore be reasonably conjectured, that the same ingenuity which planned this Church, discovered this means of ornamenting it."

---

WE must here avail ourselves of this opportunity to bring into notice the following extract from a Report of the state of the exterior of the Church, at a General Meeting of the Parishioners of Great Malvern, held on the 27th of May, 1831, at the Vestry Room.

"The roofing and the masonry of the Church, however, (then in a mouldering state,) were left untouched, as the money collected by the Reverend Vicar was no more than sufficient to defray the expences for flooring and pewing, and restoring other parts of the Church; and now, after a further lapse of fifteen years, the roof, both in its tiling and timber, is so dilapidated, that unless it is soon repaired in a substantial manner, it will threaten ruin to the whole of this venerable structure, which has so long attracted the notice and admiration of the antiquary, and of every man of taste and science. Besides the roof, the exterior walls of the nave, chancel, and side aisles require a thorough repair and fresh cementing. The battlements and pinnacles which surround the tower and the body of the Church, want new stone work. The crockets, finials, and mouldings of the exterior require to be re-sculptured; and, for the permanence of the foundation, new drains are absolutely necessary."

---

N.B. Shortly will be published the names of those Gentlemen who have already contributed their donations for the foregoing objects. In the meantime it may not be improper here to add, that Subscriptions for the repairs of the Church will be received by the following banking houses: COUTTS & Co., *Strand;* ROBARTS & Co., *Lombard Street;* and BERWICK & Co., *Worcester.*

# THE FOLLOWING WORKS

OF THE

## REV. H. CARD, D.D., F.R.S., F.A.S., M.R.S.L., F.S$^T$.S.

VICAR OF GREAT MALVERN,

ARE TO BE HAD OF

J. G. and F. RIVINGTON, 3, Waterloo Place, and St. Paul's Church Yard, and LONGMAN and Co. Paternoster Row, London; and other Booksellers.

I.
HISTORY OF THE REVOLUTIONS OF RUSSIA, in one large octavo volume. Price 12s. Second Edition. 1804.

II.
HISTORICAL OUTLINES OF THE RISE AND ESTABLISHMENT OF THE PAPAL POWER. Octavo. Price 3s. 1804.

III.
THOUGHTS ON DOMESTIC OR PRIVATE EDUCATION. Second Edition. Price 3s. 6d. 1806.

IV.
THE REIGN OF CHARLEMAGNE, considered chiefly with Reference to Religion, Laws, Literature, and Manners. Price 7s. 1807.

V.
LITERARY RECREATIONS, or ESSAYS, Moral, Historical, Religious, and Political. Second Edition. Price 8s. 1810.

VI.
BEAUFORD; or, A PICTURE OF HIGH LIFE. In two volumes. Price 15s. in boards. 1811.

VII.
TWO LETTERS ON THE SUBJECT OF TITHES. Price 4s. Second Edition. 1812. Price 2s. 6d.

VIII.
SOME OBSERVATIONS ON MR. GRANVILLE SHARP'S PLAN TO REFORM THE REPRESENTATION OF GREAT BRITAIN. 1812. Price 2s.

IX.
A LETTER CONCERNING THE OBJECTIONS MADE BY THE ANTIPÆDO-BAPTISTS TO INFANT BAPTISM. Second Edition. Price 2s. 6d. 1813.

X.
A LETTER TO WILLIAM WALL, ESQ. of Worcester, in Answer to a Publication entitled "Thoughts upon the present State of the Poor and Middling Classes of Society." Price 2s. 1817.

XI.
A DISSERTATION ON THE HEREFORDSHIRE BEACON. Price 3s. 6d. 1822.

XII.
A DISSERTATION ON THE SACRAMENT OF THE LORD'S SUPPER. Fourth Edition. Price 8s. 1823.

XIII.
A VISITATION SERMON ON THE ATHANASIAN CREED, with an Appendix and Notes. Fourth Edition. Price 2s. 6d. 1825.

XIV.
A LETTER ON THE ROMAN CATHOLIC QUESTION. 1829. Price 1s.

XV.
A LETTER ON CHURCH REFORM, with an Appendix and Notes. Third Edition. Price 3s. 1830.

XVI.
OBSERVATIONS RELATIVE TO SUFFRAGAN BISHOPS, ON THE APPOINTMENT OF AN ECCLESIASTICAL COMMISSION, AND ON CONVOCATIONS. 1831. Price 2s.

XVII.
A DISSERTATION ON THE PRINCIPAL WRITINGS OF BISHOP BURNETT. A Quarto Volume, in preparation.

**UNIVERSITY OF CALIFORNIA LIBRARY**
Los Angeles
This book is DUE on the last date stamped below.

Form L9–42m-8,'49(B5573)444

690  A dissertation on
M3C2  the antiquities
of the priory of
Great Malvern.

\*DA
690
M3C2

CPSIA information can be obtained
at www.ICGtesting.com
Printed in the USA
BVHW070917071218
535024BV00020B/917/P